Pliny the Elder and the Matter of Memory

The Roman official and intellectual Pliny the Elder's *Natural History* constitutes our primary source on the figural arts in Classical antiquity. Since the Middle Ages, Pliny's encyclopaedia has enraptured the imaginations of its readers with anecdotes and narratives about the lives and accomplishments of the great artists of the Greek past. This book explores the ways in which materials and artistic processes are constructed in *Natural History*.

In doing so, this work reflects current developments in the study of Graeco-Roman art, where the scientific analysis of sculptural stones, pigments, and metal alloys, as well as a more detailed understanding of technologies and workshop practices, has imposed radical changes in the methods and theoretical models used to approach ancient artefacts. The argument considers the role of materials in discourses on Nature, as well as their semantics and the language used to account for artistic creation. Discussion of artistic techniques addresses the discovery of resources and technologies, and the discursive implications of creation and viewing. By focusing on particular passages and exemplary case studies, this book explores the ideological, moral, and intellectual preoccupations that guide Pliny's construction of materialities and human ingenuity in a period characterised by a rapidly evolving economic landscape. The material and performative aspects of artistic, manual creation provided this early encyclopaedist with the fundaments for constructing and explaining his view of Rome's imperial mission and, more specifically, of his own strategies as a collector and recorder of 'all' the memorable facts of Nature.

This book will be of significant interest to scholars of classical archaeology, Greek and Latin literature, social and economic history, and reception studies.

Anna Anguissola teaches Classical Archaeology at the University of Pisa, Italy. Her research focuses on urban development, the relationship between Greek and Roman art, the history and techniques of ancient sculpture, and the Greek and Latin literary sources on the figural arts. She coordinates the University of Pisa's field research at Pompeii and at Hierapolis in Phrygia.

Young Feltrinelli Prize in the Moral Sciences

Roberto Antonelli, President, Class of Moral Sciences, Accademia Nazionale dei Lincei
Alberto Quadrio Curzio, President Emeritus, Accademia Nazionale dei Lincei
Alessandro Roncaglia, Joint Academic Administrator, Accademia Nazionale dei Lincei

The Accademia Nazionale dei Lincei, founded in 1603, is one of the oldest academies in the world. Since 2018 it has assigned four "Young Antonio Feltrinelli Prizes" every two years, directed to Italian researchers in the fields of moral sciences and humanities who are less than 40 years old. Each winner is then requested to write a book-length essay on their research and/or the perspectives of research in their field, directed to the general public. The Routledge Young Feltrinelli Prize in the Moral Sciences series thus includes high-quality essays by top young researchers, providing thoroughly readable contributions to different research fields. With this initiative, Accademia dei Lincei not only gives a remarkable grant to the winners of the prize in order to support their research activity, but also contributes to the international diffusion of the research of eminent young Italian scholars.

Democratizing the Economics Debate
Pluralism and Research Evaluation
Carlo D'Ippoliti

Petrarch and Boccaccio in the First Commentaries on Dante's Commedia
A Literary Canon Before its Official Birth
Luca Fiorentini

Pliny the Elder and the Matter of Memory
An Encyclopaedic Workshop
Anna Anguissola

For more information about this series, please visit: www.routledge.com/Young-Feltrinelli-Prize-in-the-Moral-Sciences/book-series/YFP

Pliny the Elder and the Matter of Memory

An Encyclopaedic Workshop

Anna Anguissola

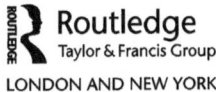

Routledge
Taylor & Francis Group

LONDON AND NEW YORK

First published 2022
by Routledge
2 Park Square, Milton Park, Abingdon, Oxon OX14 4RN

and by Routledge
605 Third Avenue, New York, NY 10158

Routledge is an imprint of the Taylor & Francis Group, an informa business

© 2022 Anna Anguissola

British Library Cataloguing-in-Publication Data
A catalogue record for this book is available from the British Library

Library of Congress Cataloging-in-Publication Data
Names: Anguissola, Anna, author.
Title: Pliny the Elder and the matter of memory :
an encyclopaedic workshop / Anna Anguissola.
Description: Abingdon, Oxon ; New York : Routledge, 2022. |
Series: Young Feltrinelli Prize in the Moral Sciences |
Includes bibliographical references and index.
Identifiers: LCCN 2021015638 (print) |
LCCN 2021015639 (ebook)
Subjects: LCSH: Artists' materials—Early works to 1800. |
Art—Early works to 1800. | Pliny, the Elder.
Naturalis historia.
Classification: LCC N8530 .A54 2022 (print) |
LCC N8530 (ebook) | DDC 709.02—dc23
LC record available at https://lccn.loc.gov/2021015638
LC ebook record available at https://lccn.loc.gov/2021015639

ISBN: 978-0-367-34988-2 (hbk)
ISBN: 978-1-032-05622-7 (pbk)
ISBN: 978-0-429-32915-9 (ebk)

DOI: 10.4324/9780429329159

Typeset in Times New Roman
by codeMantra

Contents

Figures

Preface

Written by the Roman imperial official and intellectual Pliny the Elder, the 37-book *Natural History* constitutes our primary source on the figural arts in classical antiquity. This encyclopaedia, composed of observations on the facts and materials of Nature, was published during the reign of Vespasian and is replete with information about artists and artworks, which become concentrated in the final five books. Since the Middle Ages, Pliny's 'Chapters on the History of Art', as they are colloquially known in today's scholarly debate, have enraptured the readers' imaginations with anecdotes and narratives about the lives and accomplishments of the great masters of the Greek past.

This book focuses on the ways in which materials and artistic processes are structured in the *Natural History* as a whole. In so doing, it reflects current developments in the study of Graeco-Roman art, where the scientific analysis of sculptural stones, pigments, and metal alloys, as well as a more detailed understanding of technologies and workshop practices, has imposed radical changes in the methods and theoretical models used to approach ancient artefacts. The questions explored here are the following. How is Pliny's presentation of artists and artworks affected by the perceived value, properties, and hierarchies of materials? What role do technological concerns play in the evaluation of artworks? What strategies, in terms of organisation and language, does Pliny use to reflect the complexities of these considerations? More generally, what is the place of art within the *Natural History*'s moral and epistemological framework? Finally, what challenges have materialities and human ingenuity posed to the creator of this early encyclopaedia in a period characterised by a rapidly evolving economic landscape?

The book addresses these and related questions by focusing on a set of passages from Pliny's *Natural History*, treated in individual, standalone chapters as exemplary case studies which illustrate broader issues and narratives. I argue that Pliny, by drawing attention to questions of materiality and to the process of creation and vision, reconciles the ethical imperative underpinning his narrative of Nature's facts and products with the concepts and vocabulary of a discourse on art, as well as with his distinctive interest in individual biographies. The material and performative aspects of artistic, manual creation not only occupy a central position within Pliny's narrative, but moreover provide him with the fundamentals for constructing and explaining his view of intellectual labour. This book certainly does not aim to provide a full and comprehensive reading of Pliny's encyclopaedia, or even of its final five books. It serves instead to spark further conversation regarding the role of materials in Roman discourse about, and judgement of, artworks.

The Introduction provides a brief overview of previous scholarship on Pliny the Elder's *Natural History* (and, in particular, his 'Chapters on the History of Art') and on topics instrumental to the book's argumentative arc. The Introduction covers subjects such as Pliny's political and moral standpoint, the position of art history within the treatise, and the work's organising strategies and sources.

Part I includes chapters about the properties of materials and their ethical implications, as well as about the language that Pliny uses to articulate these considerations. Chapter 1 begins with the very end of the *Natural History*, by examining the opening paragraph of Pliny's last book (*Nat.* 37.1). This paragraph not only serves to set the tone for the final volume, but also summarises key concepts developed throughout the previous sections regarding monetary value, aesthetic enjoyment, and human ingenuity. Chapter 2 explores the implications of a passage dedicated to the bronze statue of an athlete using the body-scraper (the *Apoxyomenos*) made by Lysippus, which Emperor Tiberius allegedly tried to move from its public location in Rome to his private apartment (*Nat.* 34.62). The chapter examines Pliny's argument in favour of the public utility of art and his construction of the personas of past and present emperors. Chapter 3 then investigates the language Pliny employs in discussing the figural arts. In particular, it examines the meaning and use of words such as *numerus* (rhythm), *numerosus* (rich in rhythms), and *diligentia* (assiduousness) to describe artworks, masters, and their individual style (*Nat.* 34.58). This exploration clarifies the extent to which Pliny relied on Greek sources, his manipulation of Greek technical vocabulary and its intersection with the languages of rhetoric and music.

Part II includes chapters about Pliny and his contemporaries' relationship to the processes of art: its production, understanding, and maintenance. Beginning with a close analysis of Pliny's account of artistic discoveries (*Nat.* 33.57), chapter 4 examines the role of sacred contexts in the narrative of human development. In so doing, it discusses the shifts in function and meaning that Pliny associates with a change in display contexts, notably from public to private. Chapter 5 is based on a famous passage that mentions unfinished artworks, and in particular those left incomplete following the death of their creator (*Nat.* 35.145). The chapter focuses on the meaning of *liniamenta* (sketches, projects, outlines) and returns to complicated matters of authorship, ingenuity, and falsification, which have been explored at other points in the book. Moving from an important passage regarding art's visibility in a metropolis like Rome (*Nat.* 36.27), Chapter 6 concludes the discourse regarding art's status within the urban landscape, focusing on the ways in which it was viewed and enjoyed, as well as on verbal cues that bind this discourse to a broader account of imperial ideology.

The conclusion summarises the arguments in light of the cultural climate of Flavian Rome. While the book does not make a case for Pliny's participation in or reliance upon the Roman rhetoric of the empire—a topic that has been investigated in several authoritative studies—it nonetheless demonstrates how questions regarding materials and processes, as well as the use of language, play a fundamental role in framing the *Natural History* within a broader discourse regarding the role of Rome in an increasingly globalised world.

Support towards the writing of this book has come from the Accademia Nazionale dei Lincei through an "Antonio Feltrinelli Giovani" Prize in Archaeology (2018). Research has been conducted within the framework of the Excellence Initiative of the Dipartimento di Civiltà e Forme del Sapere at the Università di Pisa. My encounter with and enthusiasm for Pliny the Elder's encyclopaedia, however, dates way earlier than this and has its roots in my time as an undergraduate student at the Scuola Normale Superiore, where Salvatore Settis and Paul Zanker first inspired me to consider questions about the ancient view of art and its impact on later scholarship. Over the years, I have enjoyed the chance to present some of the ideas discussed in this volume at various conferences and venues: the German Archaeological Institute in Rome (*Ornamenta urbis*, 2013), the Ludwig-Maximilians-Universität München (*Inter disciplinas*, 2014 and *Forms of Forgetting in Antiquity*, 2018), the Carlsberg Academy, Copenhagen (*Sacred Treasures*, 2016), the Università di Pisa (*Le parole del marmo*, 2016), the Christian-Albrechts-Universität zu Kiel (*Materiality as Decor*, 2020), and the Universität Leipzig (*Perspektiven der römischen Ikonographie*,

2019 and the International Summer School *Living in a Material World*, 2020). I am extremely grateful to the organisers and attendees of all these events, who encouraged me to develop my argument along trajectories that I would not have explored otherwise. Most importantly, it is a pleasure to acknowledge the help that I received from the friends and colleagues who read and commented on earlier drafts of the manuscript with care and generosity: Domitilla Campanile, Lucia Faedo, Leyla Ozbek, and Salvatore Settis. I am also grateful to Calla McNamee and Louise Chapman, who revised the English manuscript. Any errors and omissions are, of course, my own.

Pisa, February 2021

Editorial note and abbreviations

This volume has been designed with an interdisciplinary audience in mind. Owing to this, the names of ancient authors and the titles of their works are presented in their conventional English form, while few exceptions reflect current citation standards. The Latin text of the *Natural History* follows the Teubner edition by Karl Friedrich Theodor Mayhoff. Unless otherwise stated, all English translations from Pliny the Elder's *Natural History* are taken from the Loeb Classical Library editions. Aude Doody provides an excellent account of the extensive scholarly literature on the life and work of Pliny the Elder in a dedicated *Oxford Bibliography*, to which I refer for the many topics not covered in this book (doi: 10.1093/OBO/9780195389661-0194, last accessed 30th May 2020).

Abbreviations used in this volume for editions, translations, and commentaries of Pliny the Elder's *Natural History* (Books 33–37):

Pliny-André, Bloch, Rouveret 1981= Pline l'Ancien,
    Historie Naturelle. Livre XXXVI, ed.
    by J. André, transl. by R. Bloch, and
    commentary by A. Rouveret. Paris,
    1981 (Les Belles Lettres, Collection Budé).
Pliny-Conte 1982–1988 = Gaio Plinio Secondo,
    Storia Naturale, ed. by G.B. Conte, in
    cooperation with G. Ranucci, 5 vols.
    Torino, 1982–1988 (Einaudi, I Millenni).
Pliny-Croisille 1985 = Pline l'Ancien, *Histoire*
    Naturelle. Livre XXXV, ed., transl., and
    commentary by J.-M. Croisille. Paris,
    1985 (Les Belles Lettres, Collection Budé).
Pliny-de Saint-Denis 1972 = Pline l'Ancien, *Historie*
    Naturelle. Livre XXXVII, ed. and transl.

by E. de Saint-Denis. Paris, 1972 (Les
Belles Lettres, Collection Budé).

Pliny-Eichholz 1962 = Pliny the Elder, *Natural
History*, Books 36–37, transl. by D.E.
Eichholz. London-Cambridge MA,
1962 (Loeb Classical Library, 419).

Pliny-Ferri 2000 = Plinio il Vecchio, *Storia delle arti
antiche*, ed., transl., and commentary
by S. Ferri, with an introduction by M.
Harari. Milano, 2000 (reprinted; first
published, ed., transl., and commentary
by S. Ferri, Roma, 1946).

Pliny-Jex-Blake, Sellers 1968 = *The Elder Pliny's
Chapters on the History of Art*, transl.
by K. Jex-Blake, commentary and
historical introduction by E. Sellers.
Chicago, 1968 (reprinted; first published, London, 1896).

Pliny-König, Bayer 1989 = C. Plinius Secundus der
Ältere, *Naturkunde. Buch XXXIV*, ed.
and transl. by R. König, with K. Bayer.
München and Zürich, 1989.

Pliny-König, Hopp 2007 = C. Plinius Secundus der
Ältere, *Naturkunde. Buch XXXVI*, ed.
and transl. R. König, with J. Hopp. Düsseldorf, 2007.

Pliny-König, Hopp 2007 = C. Plinius Secundus der
Ältere, *Naturkunde. Buch XXXVII*, ed.
and transl. by R. König, with J. Hopp.
Düsseldorf, 2007.

Pliny-König, Winkler 2007 = C. Plinius Secundus
der Ältere, *Naturkunde. Buch XXXV*,
ed. and transl. by R. König, with G.
Winkler. Düsseldorf, 2007.

Pliny-Le Bonniec, Gallet de Santerre 1983 = Pline
L'Ancien, *Historie Naturelle. Livre
XXXIV*, ed. and transl. by H. Le
Bonniec, commentary by H. Gallet de
Santerre, H. Le Bonniec. Paris, 1983
(Les Belles Lettres, Collection Budé).

Pliny-Mayhoff 1875–1906 = *C. Plini Secundi
Naturalis Historiae Libri XXXVII*, ed.
by C. Mayhoff, 5 vols. Leipzig, 1875–1906.

Pliny-Rackham 1961 = Pliny the Elder, *Natural
History*, Books 33–35, transl. by H.
Rackham. London-Cambridge MA,
1961 (Loeb Classical Library, 394).
Pliny-Zehnacker 1983 = Pline l'Ancien, *Historie
Naturelle. Livre XXXIII*, ed. and transl.
by H. Zehnacker. Paris, 1983 (Les Belles
Lettres, Collection Budé).

Journals are abbreviated according to *L'Année Philologique*. Other
abbreviations:

ANRW = Temporini, H., and Haase, W. (eds.),
*Aufstieg und Niedergang der roemischen
Welt*. Berlin, 1972–
CIL = *Corpus Inscriptionum Latinarum*. 1863–
DNO = Kansteiner, S., Hallof, K., Lehmann, L.,
Seidensticker, B., and Stemmer, K.
(eds.), *Der neue Overbeck* (DNO), 5 vols.
Berlin and Boston, 2014.
EAA = *Enciclopedia dell'Arte Antica, Classica e
Orientale*, 7 vols. Roma, 1958–1966.
ILS = H. Dessau (ed.), *Inscriptiones Latinae Selectae*.
Berlin, 1892–1916.
LTUR = E.M. Steinby (ed.), *Lexicon topographicum
urbis Romae*. Roma, 1993–2000.

Introduction

Over the centuries, Pliny the Elder's dense chapters dedicated to the figural arts generated conventions and paradigms that affected the discourse on and criticism of art.[1] The *Natural History* holds a unique place as a literary text in its own right, a crucial resource to the visual culture of the classical world, and the most prolific generator of symbols, expectations, and models in the history of Western art.

Pliny's discussion of Pasiteles, one of the few artists included in the *Natural History* who lived after the age of Alexander the Great, provides an excellent example for elucidating the many ramifications of his discourse on art. Within Pliny's narrative, Pasiteles stands out as a versatile master conversant in an impressive array of materials and their usage.[2] Moreover, Pliny avails himself of Pasiteles' five volumes *de mirabilibus operibus* as a reference for lengthy sections of his encyclopaedia. Following a well-established approach to the study of ancient artists, scholars have searched the *Natural History* for information about the biography, accomplishments, and legacy of Pasiteles. A second avenue of investigation touches upon the role of Pasiteles' treatise as a source of both facts and the criteria behind their selection. Pasiteles' interest in the "famous masterpieces of the entire world" is viewed as indicative of a classicising taste that may, in turn, account for the conspicuous marginalisation of Hellenistic art in the *Natural History*.[3]

Pasiteles' engagement with *mirabilia opera* is in line with Pliny's own curiosity about the 'marvels' (*mirabilia, miracula*) of nature and human ingenuity. Emphasis on the world's 'marvels' reflects the taste and interests of Pliny's time, which arose after centuries of Roman expansion had increased the availability of resources from remote lands, fostering a keen appetite for exotic goods and knowledge.[4] In terms of Pasiteles' career, the taste for anecdotes and the citation of memorable sayings is part of a similar organising strategy. This strategy aims to dramatise historical sequences and construct immediate, relatable examples for more abstract points.[5]

Recent study of the *Natural History* stresses the close relationship between Pliny the Elder's biography, as a high-ranking official under Vespasian, and the ideological premises of his work.[6] Indeed, Pliny himself draws a direct connection between the public duties that occupy him during the day and the literary work that fills his nights (*Praef.* 18). On the one hand, his position as an imperial official afforded the competences, resources, and contacts necessary to create the encyclopaedia. On the other hand, his literary work must have provided an important outlet for reflection on his own life and career, making sense of the world and political regime in which he was deeply invested. Addressed and presented in 77 CE to future emperor Titus, the *Natural History* is essentially a large, single-minded (although not always consistent) investigation into how Nature, as an active force, unveils herself to the Roman people and the latter's ingenious experience of it.[7] From this perspective, the *Natural History* is both a product of and a guide to Roman imperial expansion.

In the *epistula praefatoria*, Pliny explains his intellectual program: to provide an "all-round education" (*Praef.* 14: ἐγκύκλιος παιδεία) made of twenty thousands "noteworthy facts".[8] He mentions using "one hundred authors" as sources and situates his work within a long-standing tradition of learned treatises and technical writings (*Praef.* 17).[9] Pliny openly claims the novelty of his 'encyclopaedic' approach (*Praef.* 1 and 14). In addition to providing a full list of sources, he discusses his treatment of them at several points.[10] Pliny is likewise explicit about his intention to include both traditional wisdom and new information (*Praef.* 15, 17; *Nat.* 14.3), concentrating on material that may be less familiar to his readers (e.g., *Nat.* 17.9). In the case of art-historical books, Pliny's many authorities include late Classical and Hellenistic treatises on sculpture and painting, as well as a variety of miscellaneous sources.[11] He must have also derived information from directly viewing the buildings and artworks of Rome, and perhaps from inscriptions or geographical maps set up in public places, as well as official lists of monuments.[12] While Pliny's research is essentially literary, he nonetheless includes remarks drawn from his own experience as often as possible.[13]

The originality of Pliny's project lies in its organising strategy. Plinian taxonomy seems to follow multiple criteria, including the narrative structure of his sources, classifications drawn from Greek philosophical thought, and associations based on analogy or antithesis.[14] At first glance, Pliny's presentation appears to follow a desultory logic that traces intertwining ethical, political, historical, and economical lines of reasoning. But closer consideration of the relationship between thematic sections and the different books leaves little doubt as to the coherence of the text's purpose and ideological premises. It is in the books dedicated to the figural arts, above all, that the *Natural History* engages explicitly with two alternative yet complementary avenues for the presentation of materials, techniques, and objects. On the one hand, Pliny is interested in constructing an image of Nature as an all-encompassing, divine, and creative force, the origin of Rome's traditional values in contrast to the greed (*avaritia*) and extravagance (*luxuria*) of the present.[15] On the other hand, the *Natural History* builds a case for the role of Rome as the place towards which all information and resources converge for the ultimate benefit of mankind. The inevitable conflict generated by these two competing perspectives stimulates the *Natural History*'s narrative tension and accounts for its seemingly erratic progress.

The relevance of the visual arts within the encyclopaedia emerges from the preface itself, where painting and sculpture serve as an explicit metaphor for the equally onerous feat of writing (*Praef.* 26, discussed in Chapter 5).[16] In the final books, Pliny introduces crafts according to their raw natural materials. Only a short section within the broader treatment of metal alloys addresses the craft of sculptors and goldsmiths. Painting features as just one of the many uses for pigments. The qualities and functions of stones are explored well beyond the field of sculpture. Overall, Pliny does not express a coherent aesthetic program. Instead, he wavers between generic appreciation of mimesis and insightful praise of the craftsman's recognition of each material's technical qualities.[17]

Pliny's preoccupation with materials and techniques is clear in the case of Pasiteles. If one focuses on the most elaborate passage that Pliny devotes to this artist (*Nat.* 35.151–156), significant details emerge to situate Pasiteles within a broader discourse on materials, their structural properties, hierarchies, and axiological associations. In order to explain both Pasiteles' work as a craftsman and his intellectualist approach to art-making, Pliny introduces his programmatic method for shaping prototypes in clay or plaster for his projects. Apparently, Pasiteles relied on a functional and conceptual sequence; he considered modelling (*plastice*, a calque of the Greek term πλαστική) as "the mother of chasing (*caelatura*), bronze statuary (*statuaria*), and sculpture in stone (*scalptura*)" (Figure I.1). On two occasions (*Nat.* 35.155–156 and 36.39–41), Pliny mentions Pasiteles together with another artist of the late-Republican period, Arcesilaus, who is also noted for his

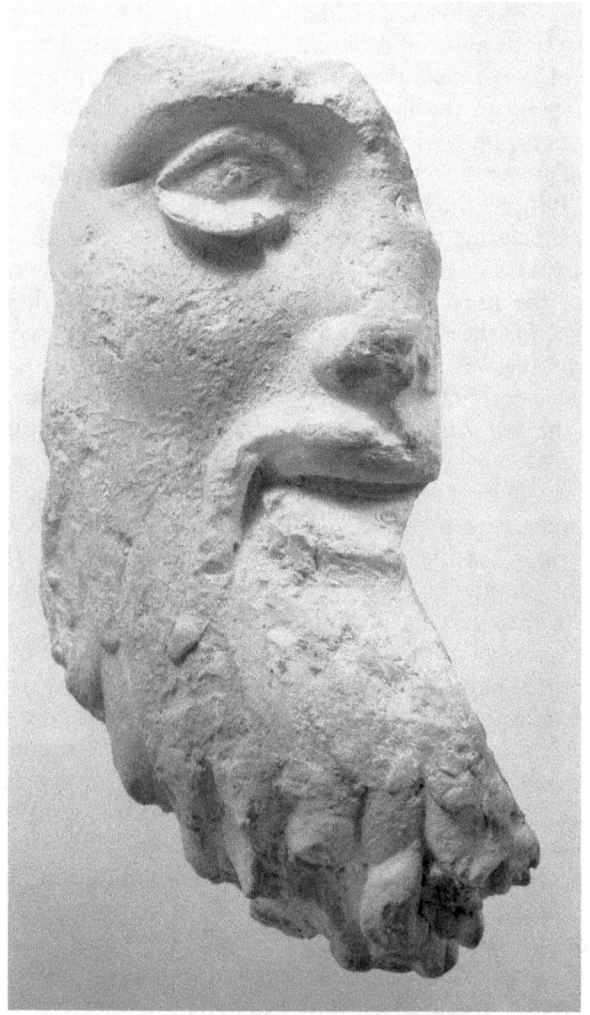

Figure I.1 Fragment of a cast used to produce copies of the statue of Aris-
togeiton, from the group of the *Tyrant-Slayers*. Plaster. H 21.6 cm;
W 10.7 cm. Baiae, Museo Archeologico dei Campi Flegrei, inv. no.
174.479.
Credit: Rome, German Archaeological Institute (D-DAI-ROM-78.1857, G. Hellner).

work in clay, marble, and perhaps even bronze. While modern readers
of Pliny are mostly fascinated with Arcesilaus' alleged skill at carving
elaborate compositions from a single block of marble, this information
bears more complex implications than traditionally assumed.[18] Like his

contemporary Pasiteles, Arcesilaus is portrayed as a craftsman whose approach to art revolved around careful consideration of technical processes (and the materials involved in them). His proficiency with marble indeed seems to depend on his preliminary designs, on the high-quality *bozzetti* that "used to sell for more, among artists themselves, than the finished works of others" (*Nat.* 35.155–156).[19] What makes the 'Chapters on the History of Art' stand out within the work is the unique opportunity they offer for investigation into the nexus of natural matter and human ingenuity. The precarious balance of this relationship becomes a prominent subject in the last book of the encyclopaedia. There, the narrative about gems and precious stones engages with questions regarding the natural creative process and Nature's ability to produce stones of exquisite shape (Figure I.2).

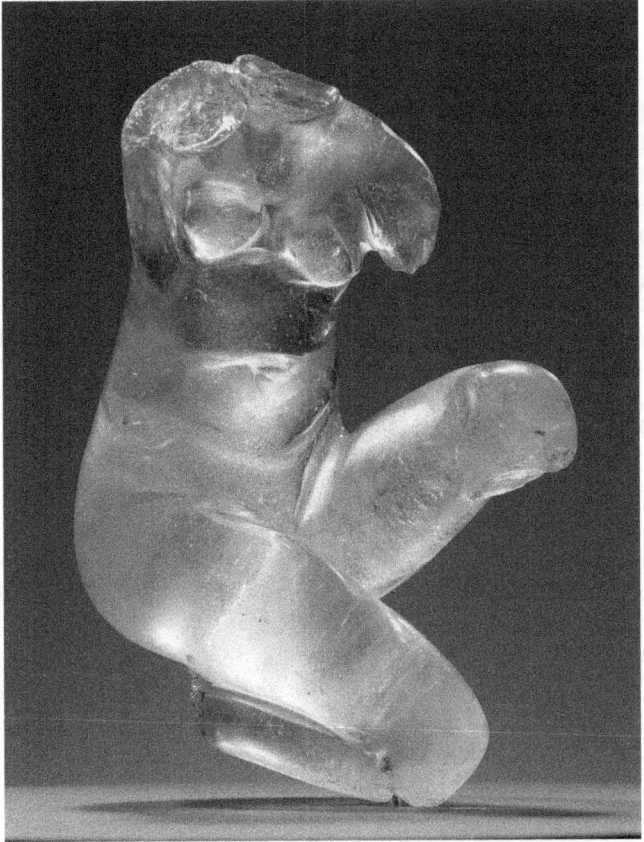

Figure I.2 Statuette of Venus, first century BCE. Rock crystal. H 8.5 cm. Malibu, The J. Paul Getty Museum, inv. no. 78.AN.248.

Credit: Los Angeles, The J. Paul Getty Museum, Open Content Programme.

In keeping with a materialistic cosmology attuned to Hellenistic and Roman Stoicism, Plinian Nature is an active, material 'breath' (*pneuma*) that pervades all matter to instil shape and causal properties according to a rational (albeit impenetrable) design.[20] Pliny opens Book 2 on cosmology by presenting the world (*mundus*) as divine (*numen*), eternal (*aeternum*), and immensurable (*inmensum*), "at once the work of Nature and Nature herself" (*Nat.* 2.1).[21] Awareness of Nature's countless, concrete manifestations provides both a subject of contemplation and a source of learning.[22] By accumulating knowledge in the course of its expansion, Rome fulfils its natural destiny; by organising this knowledge and making it available to the public, Pliny himself participates in Nature's project.

The *Natural History*'s pragmatic perspective is reflected in its presentation as a work of 'public utility' far from the idle pursuit of literary ambition or the pleasures of entertaining topics and rhetorical sophistication (*Praef.* 12 and 14).[23] Pliny invokes the principle of utility to explain the choice to provide his work with an 'index' that takes up all of Book 1 and is designed to allow readers to search for a particular fact without having to read the entire treatise (*Praef.* 33).[24] In terms of internal organisation, the *Natural History* thus seems constructed with alternative modes of consultation in mind. Both a sequential, extended reading to illuminate the overarching logic of the narrative and a narrow search for individual topics are possible. The functional and moral antithesis between 'utility' (*utilitas*) and 'pleasure' (in the *Preface: gratia, amoenitas*) is further developed towards the end of the encyclopaedia, when Pliny gets to extol the 'useful' marvels of Rome in contrast to the futile ostentation of foreign rulers.[25]

In Pliny's view, *avaritia* and *luxuria* command the cultural and economic landscape of his time. Their opposition to *utilitas*, the factual and visual expression of Rome's traditional values, runs throughout the encyclopaedia.[26] Nowhere else is the tension between these two poles—and the value systems they encapsulate—more conspicuous than in the volumes about artistic materials. There, among the primary concerns informing his narrative, Pliny seems to cultivate a delicate balance between acknowledging Nature's inviolable perfection, with its corollary of Nature-inspired 'utility', and recognising human ingenuity, which inevitably entails modification of the natural order and its substances. This point is particularly clear in the case of gold, the standard of value for all other substances (*Nat.* 33.58–60).[27] While inferior to other metals in brilliance, weight, and malleability, gold is said to owe its popularity (*gratia*) to its durability since it "loses no substance by the action of fire" and "gets extremely little worn by use". What really matters about the qualities of gold is not their relative *superiority* compared to other substances, but their *reliability* and thus the stability of their economic value. For this reason, the boundary between intrinsic (i.e., natural) and extrinsic value is particularly unstable. Considering these remarks, it is not surprising that Pliny would blame appetite for the bare material as overtaking any interest in its associated craft. In his words, it had become virtually impossible to achieve fame from engraving gold; the opposite was true for silver, the material of choice for many excellent craftsmen including Pasiteles (*Nat.* 33.154). By expressing their thoughts and creating their designs in 'humble' materials such as clay and plaster, Pasiteles and Arcesilaus proved able to escape the trappings of greed and to concentrate instead on developing their craft.

Hinting at the fate of oblivion for those who indulge in the extravagant taste of the day, Pliny seems to imply that Nature represents more than simply an ontological entity or the physical force responsible for shaping the world. For him, Nature, as the ultimate arbiter of human norms, also represents a moral principle. The power of time in re-establishing natural balance and hierarchies emerges in the section dedicated to iron. Iron is at once the most useful and most destructive substance, chosen to create helpful tools as well as deadly weapons. But "the benevolence of Nature" (*naturae benignitas*) mitigates the danger of iron over time, as this metal is extraordinarily affected by rust (*Nat.* 34.138–141). Occasionally, Nature's response to human products that defy the principle of public benefit takes a more proactive form. Thus, we see ostentatious feats such as a colossal painted portrait of Nero (*Nat.* 35.51) and the lavish homes of foolish owners being ravaged by fire (*Nat.* 36.110 and 36.115), a "vast, unruly" instrument of Nature for both creation and destruction (*Nat.* 36.201).

Throughout the six chapters that follow, this book engages with the competing narrative streams and ideological standpoints that inform the *Natural History*. It does so from the perspective of individual, yet inextricably interconnected, case studies. The argument considers the role of materials in discourses on Nature, as well as their semantics and the language used to account for artistic creation. Discussion of artistic techniques addresses the discovery of resources and technologies, and the discursive implications of creation and viewing. This book thus explores the ideological, moral, and intellectual preoccupations that guide Pliny's construction of Rome's imperial present, its past, and the role of his encyclopaedia as 'sacred storage' (*Praef.* 17) for Roman knowledge.

Notes

1 Among recent scholarship on the *Natural History*'s reception, see Doody 2010; McHam 2013; Fane Saunders 2016.
2 Pliny presents Pasiteles as an artist who worked with silver (*Nat.* 33.130, 156), stone (*Nat.* 35.156, 36.35, 39–40), bronze (*Nat.* 35.156), clay (*Nat.* 35.156), and ivory (*Nat.* 36.40), see *DNO*, nos. 3749–3755. For an account of Pasiteles' art and legacy, see La Rocca 2016 and 2017b.
3 Coulson 1976, 362–363; Gros 1978; Harari 2002; see also Pliny-Jex-Blake, Sellers 1896, lxxvii–lxxxii.
4 See Beagon 2001 and 2007; Naas 2001; 2002, esp. 244–292, 297–310, 317–321; 2004; 2011a; Carey 2003, 84–99; Mudry 2004.
5 Platt 2016a; Naas 2012a; Darab 2014a and 2014b explore the role of artists' biographies and anecdotes in the *Natural History*. On the tradition of artists' lives in the ancient world, see Rouveret 1996; Hénin and Naas 2018.
6 The fundamental references on Pliny the Elder's career remain Syme 1969 and 1987.
7 Laehn 2013, esp. 57–90 examines Pliny's encyclopaedic enterprise in light of its ideological premises, see also Naas 2002, 86–91; Murphy 2004; Doody 2010, esp. 40–91. For the relationship between encyclopaedia and imperial power, see Fear 2011. For Pliny's treatment of his sources as consequence of his social status and public role, see Murphy 2003. For excellent introductions to the ancient encyclopaedicism, its philosophical, and intellectual tradition, see König and Whitmarsh 2007; König and Woolf 2013b. For the technical treatises from the early imperial period, see also Fögen 2009.
8 On the *epistula praefatoria*, see Köves-Zulauf 1973; Pascucci 1980 and 1982; Howe 1985; Isager 1991, 18–31; Citroni Marchetti 1991, 15–21; Sinclair 2003; Schultze 2011, 167–169; Fögen 2013, 85–93; Fuhrer 2014, 227–233; Roche 2016.
9 On the history and meaning of the phrase ἐγκύκλιος παιδεία, see Mette 1960; Vial-Logeay 2017, 25–26. Quintilian (*Institutes of Oratory* 1.10.1) uses the same words to indicate a general education, viz. as a propaedeutic to more advanced studies. For Pliny's models and the encyclopaedic genre, see Citroni Marchetti 1991, esp. 30–49, and 1992; Healy 1999, 42–62; Naas 2002, 16–27, and 2013, 145–159; Carey 2003, 17–40; Doody 2009; Conte 2012.
10 E.g., *Nat.* 3.1 e 7.8. On Pliny's sources, see Naas 2002, 137–170 (as well as 107–136 for Pliny's working methods); Ferraro 1975. Several works address his sources on individual topics (e.g., Fögen 2013 on Books 2, 14, and 25) and his approach to certain authorities (e.g., Fögen 2010a on Aristotle and Cato the Elder). On Pliny's treatment of his sources and the creation of autorial distance, see also Serbat 1973. Naas 2002, 81–84 and Carey 2003, 20–26 discuss the ways in which Pliny constructs a sense of completeness and asserts control over his project and sources.

11 See Becatti 1951, 54–56; Naas 1996; Melina 2007, Rouveret 2007. On Xenocrates, see Schweitzer 1932; E. Sellers in Pliny-Jex-Blake, Sellers 1968,
xvi–xxxvi; Pliny-Le Bonniec, Gallet de Santerre 1983, 49–54; Koch 2000,
121–127; Harari 2000a, 11–14. For Duris of Samos, see Naas 2016 and Landucci 2009, both with earlier literature. For Antigonus of Carystus, see
Dorandi 2019, with earlier literature.
12 See La Regina 1991, as well as the classic treatment in Hauser 1905.
13 See the comments in Lloyd 1983, 136–140.
14 The best account of Plinian taxonomy is Lao 2016 (esp. 213–224 about
earlier literature); see also Conte 1982 and 2012; Della Corte 1982; Locher
1986; Naas 2002, 171–234; Carey 2003, 26–30; Murphy 2004, 29–48; Li
Causi 2010; Henderson 2011; Naas 2019. For the organisation of Books
34–37, see Isager 1991, 109–113, 206–209.
15 Wallace-Hadrill 1990, esp. 81, 92.
16 On the place of art history in Pliny's encyclopaedia, see Isager 1991; Naas
2002, 95–105; Carey 2003; Tanner 2006, 235–246; Citroni Marchetti 2019.
17 See Carey 2003, 105–111; Isager 1991, 136–139. For 'interpretive commu-
nities' of viewers (and for 'popular' or 'professional' aesthetics) in the ancient world, see Hardiman 2012; Perry 2005, 18–22.
18 *Nat.* 36.34, 36, 37, 41. The mention of works made *ex uno lapide* seems to be
a conventional form of praise rather than an observation based on reality;
elsewhere Pliny marvels at objects created in such a way that they appear
made of a single block of their substance (*Nat.* 13.93), see Anguissola 2018,
168–171; Settis 1999, 49–50, 79–81.
19 In both cases, Pliny's source is Varro (who was apparently a keen admirer
of the artists from Pasiteles' circle). For Varro's taste and understanding
of art, see Becatti 1951, 63–72. Varro's role as a source for Pliny is explored
by H. Gallet de Santerre in Pliny-Le Bonniec, Gallet de Santerre 1953,
54–55; see also E. Sellers in Pliny-Jex-Blake, Sellers 1896, lxxxii–lxxxv. For
Arcesilaus, see *DNO*, nos. 3739–3742; A. Corso in Pliny-Conte 1982–1988,
V, 481, 483, 599, 601, 873.
20 On Roman Stoicism, see Già Comella 2014.
21 For Pliny's idea of Nature, see Beagon 1992, 62–64, 92–102; see also Beagon 1996 for his construction of landscape and Vegetti 1981 on 'Nature
as spectacle' in the *Natural History*. On Pliny's philosophical perspective,
see Isager 1991, 32–47; Citroni Marchetti 1991, 21–30 and 1992; Paparazzo
2011. On aspects of Pliny's concept of 'god' (as expressed, e.g., in *Nat.* 2.14–
27), see Dumont 1986.
22 Doody 2013, 291.
23 See also *Nat.* 28.2. See Naas 2002, 84–86; Beagon 2013.
24 See Doody 2001 and 2010, 92–131. See also Naas 2002, 171–195, 262–271;
Riggsby 2007, 93–98.
25 See Naas 2004 and 2011a.
26 This antithesis is explicit, for instance, in the case of amber: *Nat.* 37.30
and 49. For Pliny's place in the Roman moralising discourse, see Citroni
Marchetti 1982 and 1991. For his criticism of greed and extravagance,
see Wallace-Hadrill 1990, 85–92; Isager 1991, 52–55, 70–73; Beagon 1992,
75–79; Carey 2003, 76–79; Cotta Ramosino 2004, 251–270; Murphy 2004,
96–99. For an overview of the concept of luxury in Roman society, see
Berry 1994, 63–86.

27 See also *Nat.* 33.42–47 and 62. In the closing section of the treatise, Pliny remarks that, however universally employed as a standard of value, gold only ranks tenth in the hierarchy of the most precious natural substances (*Nat.* 37.204). On the place of gold in Pliny's hierarchy of materials, see Anguissola, forthcoming.

Part I
The nature of art

1   Art and material

Ut nihil instituto operi desit, gemmae supersunt et in artum coacta rerum naturae maiestas, multis nulla parte mirabilior. Tantum tribuunt
varietati, coloribus, materiae, decori, violare etiam signis, quae causa
gemmarum est, quasdam nefas ducentes, aliquas vero extra pretia
ulla taxationemque humanarum opum arbitrantes, ut plerisque ad
summam absolutamque naturae rerum contemplationem satis sit una
aliqua gemma.

(*Natural History* 37.1)

In addition to setting the tone for the discussion of gems and precious
stones, the first paragraph of Pliny's last volume summarises many
essential points of the encyclopaedia.[1] Gems, Pliny argues, deserve a
place above all other materials in terms of both monetary and aesthetic
value, as masterpieces of variety (*varietas*), colour (*color*), texture
(*materia*), and beauty (*decor*).[2] It is owing to this intrinsic perfection
that many consider it a crime (*nefas*) to tamper with (*violare*) certain
types of stones by engraving them as signets. A single gemstone alone
is sufficient to provide "a supreme and perfect aesthetic experience
of the wonders of Nature" (*ad summam absolutamque naturae rerum
contemplationem*). Despite their diminutive size, gems encapsulate and
showcase the magnificence (*maiestas*) of Nature, which Pliny painstakingly describes over his 36 books dedicated to cosmology, anthropology, animals, vegetation, and minerals.

Scholars have noted that lengthy introductions and conclusions
cluster towards the end of the treatise, likely owing to the work's
increasing complexity, interrelatedness, and awareness of purpose.[3] In
the case of gemstones, the opening paragraph is also responsible for
detailing new categories of classification and evaluation, which have
rarely been employed in previous books. In the chapters regarding

DOI: 10.4324/9780429329159-1

gems and precious stones, intrinsic qualities—perceived through the senses—emerge as indispensable tools for appraising, criticising, and ranking objects and materials. The senses are the sole instruments for understanding substances that elude all efforts at intellectual rationalisation. We may argue that the *Natural History* presents gemstones as a synthesis of both Nature's properties and the methods used to describe and classify them. The rest of the natural world serves as a comparison: a familiar reference to describe what is often otherwise indefinable.[4] The idea of the ultimate untouchability of precious stones expresses a tension between natural properties (*materia*) and artistic skill (*ars*) that runs throughout the encyclopaedia. Commercial value (*pretium*), which, in Pliny's work, often hangs in the balance between the competing factors of material worth and artistic skill, is explicitly excluded in the discussion of gems. As the perfect product of Nature, gems defy the bounds and preoccupations of human economy.

A key concern in the opening paragraph of Book 37 is the power of reduction and concentration. The greatness of Nature has been condensed (*coacta*) into each individual gem, to the point that the inspection (*contemplatio*) of a single stone can provide an immersive, all-encompassing aesthetic experience. This is an increasingly central aspect of Pliny's final volumes, where the concentration of marvels in certain places implicitly mirrors Pliny's own collection of facts.[5] At the very end of the work, before saluting the object of his investigation and the "mother of all creation", Nature, Pliny returns to the place where all the world's resources converge: Italy. He then enumerates a list of the most prized creatures and substances (*Nat.* 37.201–204).

This chapter argues that the treatment of gemstones provides a compendium of the concepts and beliefs outlined throughout the entire encyclopaedia, while at the same time experimenting with new strategies for classification about an extraordinarily challenging subject. How does the conclusion clarify and systematise thoughts developed in earlier sections of the treatise? What is the place of gemstones among the products of Nature and what categories does Pliny employ to account for their variety and for the position they occupy in human imagery? How, moreover, does a 'taxonomy of the senses' contribute to this double effort of classification and theoretical salience?

Natural art

In several respects, the last two volumes constitute a cluster within the *Natural History*. Both concern stones, albeit of different sizes, availabilities, and values. More to the point, both highlight the same preoccupation with *gaze*, and the concentration of resources or qualities in a single object or place (and, implicitly, in a single work of literature). Pliny harmonises the passage between the two volumes, moving away from building stones in the final section of Book 36 to concentrate on 'liminal' materials with reflective properties, like glass (*Nat.* 36.189–195) and obsidian (*Nat.* 36.196–198). Glass occupies an important place in the broader treatment of gemstones, as both a familiar term of comparison for the quality of transparency and the chief substance used for the falsification of gems.[6] The position of obsidian between stones and gems is even more precarious (Figure 1.1). Owing to its similarity with glass, Pliny feels that it is proper to address obsidian at this point in his work, instead of accounting for it much later, amongst other black stones (*Nat.* 37.177). Pliny's apparent need to explain his criteria reflects an awareness that the classification of obsidian may constitute a controversial issue. Obsidian is introduced in light of its affinity with, and difference from, glass (*Nat.* 36.196).[7] The best glass is in turn as translucent and colourless as rock crystal (viz. quartz; *Nat.* 36.198), the first stone introduced in the following volume. Following glass and obsidian, Book 36 closes with a substance that holds an intermediate position between all other materials and Nature herself: fire (*Nat.* 36.200–204). While everything that has been described until this point "depends upon Man's talent for making Art reproduce Nature" (*Nat.* 36.200), fire escapes the distinction between producer and product, acting as a "vast, unruly" force and an instrument for creation (*Nat.* 36.201).[8] From this point onwards, and throughout the last book of the *Natural History*, the role of human ingenuity is largely irrelevant, being limited to the falsification of gems.

The first two materials discussed in the final volume of the encyclopaedia, fluorite or fluorspar and rock crystal, present close affinities with glass, which is used for the falsification of both (*Nat.* 37.18–30).[9] Fluorite or fluorspar is mined in a variety of colours and is used to create the so-called 'myrrhine vases'. Although allegedly created by counterpoised natural circumstances, and obtained from the earth using different methods, 'myrrhine' and rock crystal share the feature of fragility, which is also the main reason for their popularity (*Nat.* 35.5).[10] Both were carved into delicate and expensive drinking vessels, with 'myrrhine' employed for cold and hot drinks, while rock crystal could not withstand heat and was used exclusively for cold liquids (*Nat.* 37.26, 30).[11]

Pliny associates the alleged differences in a material's tolerance to various conditions and temperatures with the alleged mode of formation. Rock crystal is considered as some sort of extraordinarily hard

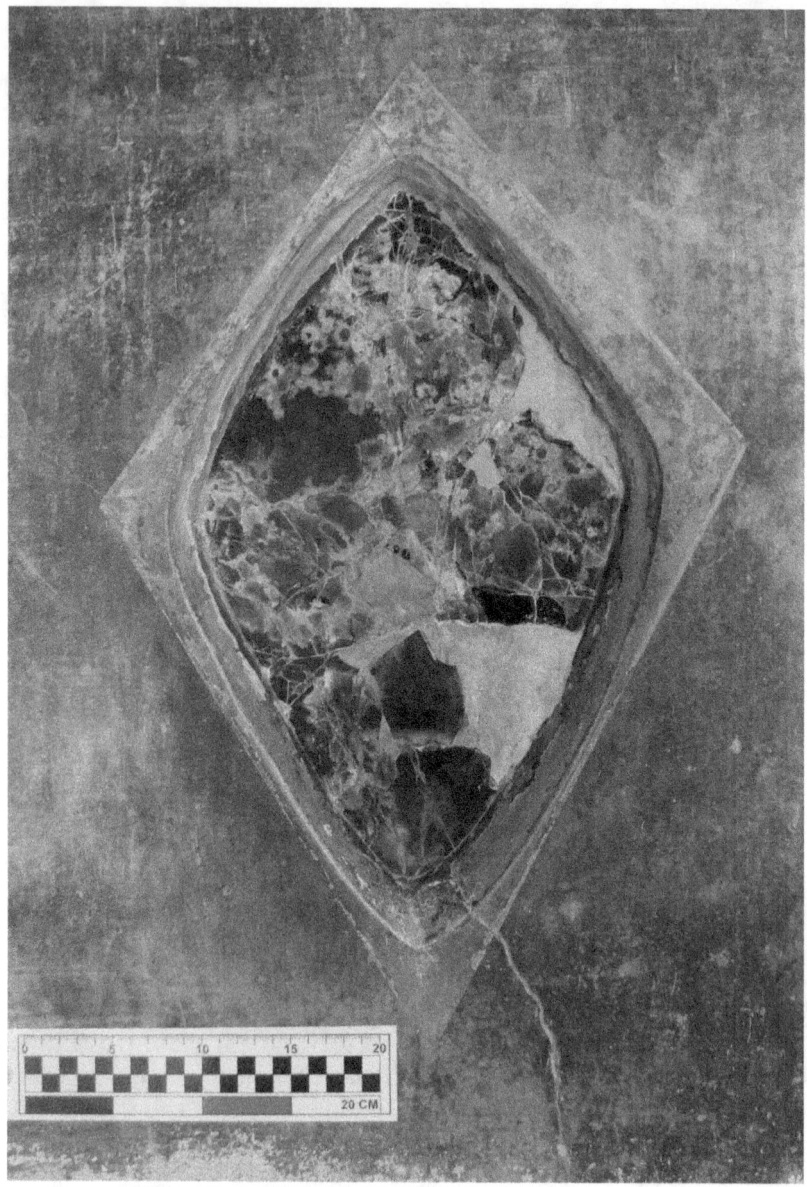

Figure 1.1 Pompeii, obsidian 'mirror' in the peristyle of the House of the
Golden Cupids (VI 16, 7.38), Fourth Style (62–79 CE). Max. H 39.5
cm; max. W 24.5 cm.

Credit: Author.

and compact ice (*Nat.* 37.23), that is, as hyper-condensed water. This intrinsically reversible state explains the material's inability to withstand heat.[12] By accounting for the behaviour of natural substances based on patterns of 'homeopathic affinities', Pliny reveals his commitment to the doctrine of cosmic sympathy (συμπάθεια), which has its roots in Stoic materialism. Sympathy is a function of the vital force (*pneuma*) that infuses all matter, holding the natural world in a state of interdependence. The principles of sympathy and antipathy govern Pliny's presentation of the vegetal, animal, and mineral world as an overarching explanation for affinities and contrasts.[13]

The formation of gems follows a common paradigm. Gems are a petrification of an originally liquid substance, formed from a reaction between opposing external forces, such as cold and heat.[14] In the case of rock crystal, the relationship between its 'liquid past' and 'solid present' is implicitly unstable. A fascination with the formation of rock crystal is a well-established *topos* in Hellenistic and Roman visual culture.[15] In Posidippus' third-century BCE collection of poems about stones (known as *lithika*), the epigram dedicated to rock crystal is placed after those on carved gems, which display superlative artistic prowess (*Epigram* 16 AB).[16] Unlike the latter, rock crystal is presented as a rough product of Nature, torn from a mountain and brought to the seashore in a "vast quantity of chunks" by the raging stream of a river.[17] A much later source—the late-antique poet Claudian—provides a more elaborate, and sensually richer, account of the hybrid nature of rock crystal.[18] In a series of seven short epigrams (33–39), Claudian describes the miracle of a drop of water included in a piece of crystal, the residual effect of imperfect crystallisation (*Epigram* 33) and an indication of the material's original identity.[19] The contrast between the icy, hard stone and the liquid substance 'imprisoned' underneath its surface elicits an irresistible sensual reaction (*Epigram* 38). Claudian depicts the excitement of children touching the chilly mass, emphasising the contrast of their soft hands (*tenero pollice*) rubbing the hardness of the stone (*marmore*), and their eager lips pressing onto the dry surface, in the hope of tasting the water beneath.

Throughout Pliny's final book, the inclusion of other things or creatures in a precious stone is a common motif that is used to explain both the optical appearance of a certain substance and its process of formation. Often, Pliny describes the ineffable brightness of a stone as containing a real source of light—a star, a flame, or the moon itself.[20] Similarly, the quality of reflection is connected to the presence of an eye or a pupil inside the stone, looking outside and engaging both natural light and the viewer's gaze.[21] Pliny corroborates the origin of amber as "liquid exudation", citing the occasional incorporation into the stone of insects "that may have remained trapped inside it as it hardened" (*Nat.* 37.46).[22] The frequency with which Roman intaglios indeed represent the outlines of small insects—as if emerging from underneath the stone's surface—attests to the widespread popularity of discourse about the generation of gems and their interaction with living creatures (Figure 1.2). In the *Natural History*, however, the relationship between gems and insects is constructed at a much deeper level. Both categories are a testament to Nature's skill as a craftsman, serving as evidence of her *maiestas* "gathered together within the narrowest limits" (*Nat.* 37.1) and her perfection beyond words (*Nat.* 11.2, speaking about insects).[23] Bees, in particular, constitute an awe-inspiring

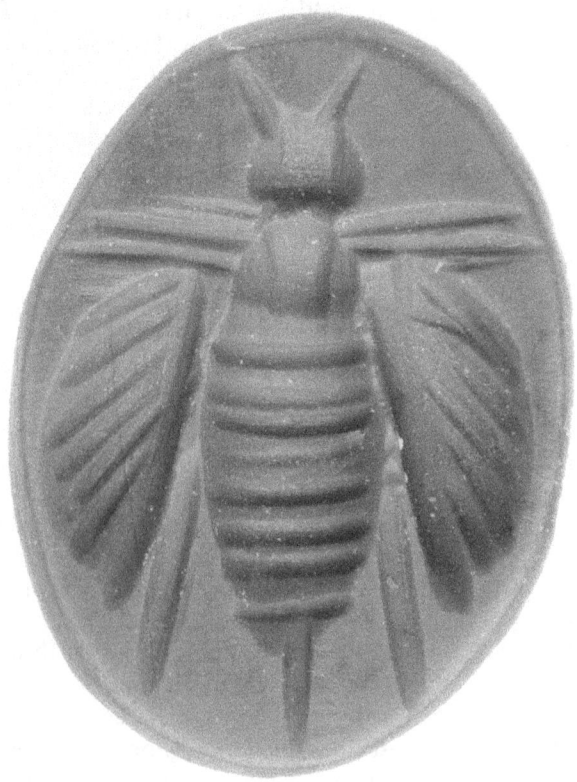

Figure 1.2 Oval gem with a bee, Roman imperial period. Jasper. L 8 mm. Boston, Museum of Fine Arts, acc. no. 1972.964.

Credit: Boston, Museum of Fine Arts.

collection of qualities, capabilities, and productivity within a "tiny ghost of an animal" (*Nat.* 11.12).[24]

The last volume of the encyclopaedia highlights the creative role of Nature, placing Man in the position of spectator or, at most, the entity who recognises the potential of Nature's work and adapts it to use. Rock crystal's naturally perfect smooth faces (*Nat.* 37.26: *absolutus laterum levor*), meeting at six corners, pose a challenge to both human reason (*non facile ratio iniri potest*) and ingenuity due to man's inability to imitate this marvel (*ut nulla id arte possit aequari*).[25] Other stones emerge from the earth as hexagonal, cubic, globular, and heart-shaped.[26] In one case—reinforcing the connection to insects, and, in particular, to the most elaborate of them all, the bee—Pliny states that the stone called 'crocallis' mirrors exactly the cells of a honeycomb (*Nat.* 37.154), thus echoing an earlier passage that describes the architecture of a beehive (*Nat.* 11.20–29). Extraordinarily organised societies of bees operate in military camps (*more castrorum*) with gates, houses, palaces, workshops, and storage rooms—all created by sequences of hexagonal cells, "each side being made by one of the bee's six feet" (*Nat.* 11.29). The form of the bee's environment is a direct expression of that animal's anatomy and, as such, a forthright manifestation of Nature's creative rationale and worldly interconnection.

The practice of leaving particularly exquisite stones untouched, to which Pliny refers in the opening paragraph of Book 37, evidences a recognition of the value of these materials, as well as the supremacy of their divine craftsman.[27] In the case of rock crystal, which serves as an exemplum for many of Pliny's claims, engraving is recommended only to disguise small blemishes and impurities (*Nat.* 37.28). Perfect pieces (*sine vitio*)—the colour of limpid water—are left unengraved (*pura*). A block of rough crystal of fabulous weight (a 'large chunk' like the πολλὴ βῶλος praised by Posidippus, *Epigram* 16 AB) is indeed reported to have been treated as an artwork in its own right in Rome and dedicated by Livia, Augustus' wife, in the Capitol (*Nat.* 37.27). Indeed, throughout Book 37, the role of man as a maker of objects and artworks is, at best, limited. Unlike the works of art cited in the foregoing volumes, gems exist outside of human time and are independent from men's creative endeavours.[28] Pliny's exploration of this concept, which occupies a peripheral position in his Hellenistic sources, provides an insightful example of the *Natural History*'s originality, as well as of Pliny's philosophical and ideological preoccupations.

Nonetheless, the ambiguities that are intrinsic to the relationship between the work of Nature and human ambition, especially the social practices of his contemporaries, did not escape Pliny's keen eye. In his discussion of signet rings (*Nat.* 33.22), Pliny presents engraved gems as a consequence of immoderate opulence (*luxuria*), and the source of fundamental confusion between material value (*materia*) and artistic quality (*ars*), which constitute contrasting and competing parametres in a hierarchy ruled by aspirational consumption. In his words, the same appetite for extravagance is responsible for the widespread idea that engraving certain gems is sacrilegious (*violari nefas putavit*), and that they should be worn whole (*solidas*), so as "to prevent anybody's imagining that people's finger-rings were intended for sealing documents". While expressed in strikingly similar terms, the point made here could not be more distant from what Pliny implies at the beginning of the book on gems, that choosing to avoid engraving certain gems is the sign of a respectful attitude towards the superior intelligence of Nature.[29] Indeed, within the framework of Pliny's conflicting views regarding the historical *present*, the ideologically laden *past*, and the *perennial* immanence of Stoic *pneuma*, both positions are justified. The key to understanding this inconsistency is Pliny's emphasis on the *functional* reason for having gems set into a ring, which is to use them as seals. Although mesmerised with the perfection of certain pieces, Pliny remains aware of his work's mission, as a reference about the 'correct' use of substances within an industrious and purposeful society. The respect for Nature and the imperative of utility coexist in two complementary dimensions of the encyclopaedia.

The art of classification

After his short section on marble sculpture, Pliny issues a warning about his selective criteria for the remainder of Book 36 (*Nat.* 36.54): he vows not to list all kinds and colours of marble, both because they are too varied (*in tanta multitudine*) and because the subject is already well known to his readers. In the following volume, instead, Pliny embarks upon a painstakingly detailed inventory of gems and precious stones, based largely on their appearance.[30] In order to classify hundreds of items, Pliny consistently resorts to nuances in qualities such as colour, transparency, clearness, and brilliance, expressed by analogy with, or in contrast to, other substances and living creatures. The challenges with this approach emerge in the presentation of opals (*Nat.* 37.80–81), introduced by the puzzling comment that they are at once very similar to, and strikingly different from, beryls, which Pliny had discussed in the previous paragraphs. The difficulty in describing opals lies in their many analogies to other stones, thereby enabling an intricate nexus of comparisons: from the hue of emeralds and amethysts, to the colour of the pigment azurite, to the brilliance of the *carbunculus*, and even to a fire stoked with olive oil.

Pliny's frustration with the elusiveness of his subject mirrors his readers' discomfort with a method for classification that seems to rest on similarities and differences in the perception of intrinsically ambiguous features. A closer look at the organisation of the text and the patterns of comparison, however, reveals the conceptual consistency of Pliny's approach. In order to clarify this point, we return to the passage regarding the opal, and move backwards in the treatise to follow the chain of comparisons with emeralds and beryls. The sequence begins with emeralds. Pliny devotes three paragraphs to itemising the physical qualities and optical effects of these stones (*Nat.* 37.62–64). The intensity of their "mellow green colour" is said to surpass that of young plants and leaves, and the way in which they transmit light is redolent of water.[31] Emeralds possess other important physical features: they are "concave in shape", "shine gently", and "reflect their colour upon the air around them". Later in the treatise, we learn that beryls share fundamental features (*natura*) with emeralds, as well as the same defects (*Nat.* 37.76–79). Pliny concentrates on the strategies employed by stone-cutters in order to enhance the reflective properties of beryls. In learning that opals differ "very little, and also very considerably" from beryls, the reader can form an idea of the new stone based on the information provided in the sections leading up to this point, all the way back to the gentle green and water-like hue of emeralds.[32]

In order to encapsulate his protean subject, with which many of his readers would have been unacquainted, Pliny relies on evoking the viewing process of gems as compared to the sensory experiences with other substances. This strategy aligns with the prescriptions of Aristotelian optics (*On the Soul* 418a–419a), based on the interaction of four main factors: the eye, a body made visible by colour (the stone), the medium (transparent air, which "colour is capable of setting in motion"), and some form of illumination, since "the colour of each thing is always seen in light".[33] In Book 37, the notion of transparency (under which heading the classical tradition includes translucency and a variety of other intermediate conditions) constitutes—together with colour—the physical quality that allows an object to respond to light.[34] Geometry moreover plays a crucial role in the effort to account for each gem's reflectance. Pliny's insistence on the shape of regular prisms or smooth cylinders reveals his (as well as his sources') preoccupation with the phenomena of reflection, along with an awareness of the laws of optics (Figure 1.3).[35] When discussing beryls, Pliny explicitly connects their shape to their reflectance, and thus to the

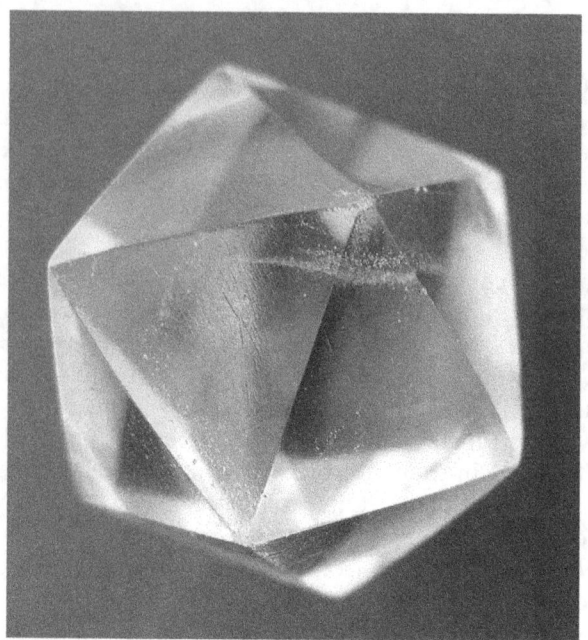

Figure 1.3 Icosahedron (regular polyhedron with 20 faces) from Rome, early
        first century CE. Rock crystal. Distance from the edges 28.47 mm,
        weight 21.6 g. Berlin, Antikensammlung, inv. no. 30891ss.
Credit: Antikensammlung, Staatliche Museen zu Berlin – Preussischer Kulturbesitz.

visual experience that they afford (*Nat.* 37.76, 78–79). Although Pliny
explains towards the end of the volume (*Nat.* 37.196) that concave or
convex stones (*cavae aut extuberantes*) are deemed to be of lesser value
than those with a plane surface, in several other places he stresses the
importance of these features as a tool for visual optimisation. Convex
surfaces are instrumental to the view of a stone's core (*Nat.* 37.88),
while a concave shape concentrates the vision, transforming the gem
into a lens (*Nat.* 37.64).[36] Pliny's classification abandons the historical
narrative on which large sections of his previous books rely. Independent of human ingenuity (the role of which is limited to figuring out
how to perceive or enhance their features), gems belong to the sphere
of natural phenomena, placed outside time and only incidentally connected to the vicissitudes of men.

Sensual matters

The description of emeralds is exemplary of Pliny's interest in the evocation of sensory experience as a means for organising gemstones into a hierarchy (*Nat.* 37.62–64).[37] The *auctoritas* of these stones derives from the "pleasing appearance" of their colour, as well as a myriad of extraordinary visual effects. They satisfy the eye without overwhelming it, restore sight, and function as lenses thanks to their concavity. Owing to the ease with which light can pass through them (*ad crassitudinem sui facilitate tralucida*), emeralds shine gently and "reflect their colour upon the air around them" to the point that they appear larger when perceived from a distance. It is due to these properties that men seem to have reached a tacit agreement not to engrave emeralds, opting instead to preserve them as Nature intended.

Throughout Book 37, the haptic features of objects occupy a central place, in line with the sensualistic approach to gemstones characterising the Hellenistic tradition.[38] In addition to resorting to colour as the main criterion for his catalogue, Pliny explores its effects on the human eye. This typically occurs by means of comparison with plants and flowers.[39] It appears that the chief facet of a colour's agreeableness is its stability, that is, the duration of the experience it affords the viewer. While praising the gentle, mellow colour of an amethyst, which "does not [...] dazzle the eye" (*Nat.* 37.122), Pliny is less impressed with a stone named hyacinth (*Nat.* 37.125), which is of a similar hue but is diluted to such an extent that "although at first sight the colour is agreeable, it loses its power before we can take our fill of it" (*evanescit antequam satiet*).[40] Hyacinth is as ephemeral as its namesake flower. With regard to verdant stones, Pliny articulates their sensory qualities in further detail, arguing for their restoring, soothing powers.[41] Staring at emeralds (*Nat.* 37.62–63) proves to be even more pleasing than gazing at grass and leaves. Their soothing power is such that Pliny recommends emeralds as a remedy for eye strain. It seems that the value of emeralds, which Pliny also characterises as being mostly concave in shape and thus able to "concentrate the vision", coincides with the sensory experience they afford. Emeralds are not merely stones to look *at*; they are stones *for* looking. Pliny's account of the properties of emeralds harkens back to Aristotelian optics.[42] According to Aristotle (*Problems* 959a), green objects are only moderately solid and thus partake in one essential feature of liquid substances, viz. allowing sight to rest quietly on their permeable surface. This line of reasoning explains why green emeralds may be thought to possess healing powers, such that they were purportedly used as optical devices.[43] Rather than being a mere object of experience, the 'vibrant matter' of Pliny's gemstones influences and steers human perception, acting as an instrument for sensual experience.[44]

Pliny does not rely on sight alone to convey an impression of proximity to his material. In his account, the properties of gems are often activated by touch. Rubbing a stone may release its heat (*Nat.* 37.189) and smell (*Nat.* 37.43), unleash its powers of attraction (*Nat.* 37.48, 103–104), soften its glow (*Nat.* 37.99), and produce a liquid perspiration (*Nat.* 37.162, 170). Touch and taste help to distinguish a gem's chill from the warmth of a counterfeit (*Nat.* 37.128, 199). A pleasant smell counts among the reasons that make certain stones praiseworthy (*Nat.* 37.22, 47, 147, 149, 185). The classification of gems in analogy to other substances occasionally relies upon their scent (*Nat.* 37.43, 145, 174) and taste (*Nat.* 37.157, 162, 173).[45] Finally, the affinity with metals, which often emerges in the reflective quality of surfaces, depends, in one case, on a stone's tinkling (*Nat.* 37.154). In evoking a web of interrelations between different things and substances, the senses connect men to the many, otherwise innumerable products of Nature.

In order to fully engage with a stone and perceive its qualities, Pliny recommends that we examine it from specific angles or at certain times of day.[46] When tilting the white stone known as 'asteria' ("star stone"), a light seems to oscillate within it, responding to movement like the pupil of an eye (*Nat.* 37.131). Thanks to the imagery of the eyes, which Pliny consistently associates with gems, he characterises these materials as susceptible to the human touch and gaze, interacting with viewers in a synaesthetic dialogue. A fascination with the idea of gems having eyes of their own—able to engage with the observer—may explain the Roman taste for stones with concentric rings, which create abstract, eye-like patterns (Figure 1.4).[47] That stones may possess some elemental, sensuous facets is made especially clear in the case of magnets, which bring to tangible extremes the principle of *sympathia* regulating the affinities between different creatures and objects. Pliny dwells extensively on the ability of certain stones not only to *attract* other materials, but to interact with the environment by irradiating their colour into air and water, as well as any adjoining objects.[48]

Pliny's interest in the interplay between stone and air first emerges in the volume on marble and other non-precious stones. Occasionally, he refers to the brilliance of a statue (*Nat.* 36.32: *marmoris radiatio*), which is so intense that those intending to stare at it (*in cuius contemplatione*) are invited to protect their eyes (*parcere oculis*). In particular, the sensory reconstruction of inner spaces seems expedient to the

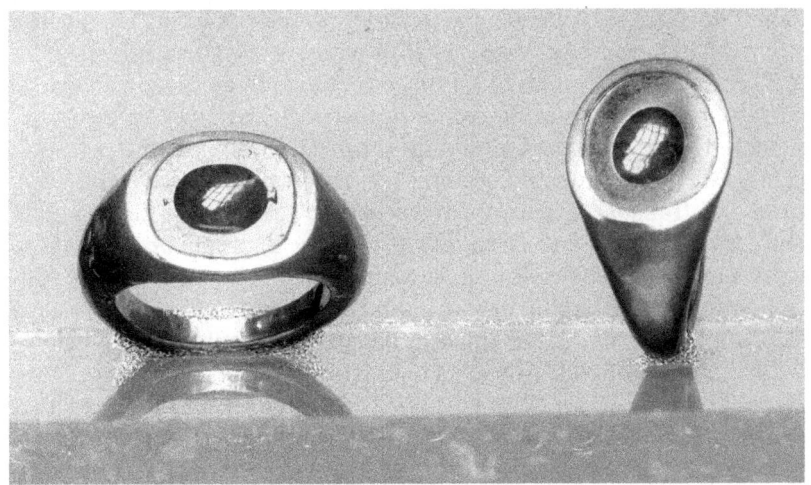

Figure 1.4 Gold rings with precious stones, early first century CE. Stone 1.41
× 1.19 cm. Berlin, Antikensammlung, inv. nos. 7075, 7076.
Credit: Antikensammlung, Staatliche Museen zu Berlin – Preussischer Kulturbesitz.

presentation of categories destined to become crucial a few paragraphs
ahead. Although generally oblivious to the decorative dimension of
the built environment, Pliny is occasionally keen to describe the experience of visiting a temple's cell. For instance, he praises the spectacu-
lar visual effects created by gold in the interior of a shrine at Cyzicus
(*Nat.* 36.98). A thin thread of gold was inserted into every vertical joint
of the stonemasonry, so that very fine filaments of light could shine
through the marble interstices, and a warm, gentle reflection could
dance upon the statues' surface. The account of this temple at Cyzicus
depends on sources of questionable reliability,[49] but Pliny must have
had direct experience of a building in Rome that evoked a similar impression. He reports (*Nat.* 36.163) that during Nero's principate a new
type of stone was discovered in Cappadocia, one that was hard, white,
and translucent (*lapis duritia marmoris, candidus atque tralucens*). This
material, called *phengites*, was used to rebuild the Temple of Fortuna,
incorporated by the Emperor in his palace (*amplexus aurea domo*).[50]
Thanks to the translucent stone, the Temple's interior enjoyed permanent illumination (*claritas* [...] *diurna*). Pliny, however, remarks
upon the difference between *phengites* and the so-called *lapis specularis* (reflective stone) discussed immediately before (*Nat.* 36.160–162),
which is thought to derive its properties from its formation process,

similar to that of rock crystal. While *lapis specularis* allows light to penetrate from the outside and irradiate (*transmissa*), in Nero's new stone the light remained trapped within its surface (*inclusa*).

These passages exemplify Pliny's method of connecting various parts of the encyclopaedia, while in fact focusing each time on particular ethical, historical, and philosophical questions. In the case of gems, Pliny's attempts to highlight the optical qualities of colour, texture, and transparency are instrumental in reaffirming the image of Nature at the very end of the treatise as the supreme *artifex*, whose work surpasses and defies human effort, while being inextricably connected to men through a network of sensual experiences. The discussion of light-flooded inner spaces in Book 36, by contrast, articulates a disparate set of concerns. The temple of Fortuna 'appropriated' by Nero within his *Domus Aurea* provides yet another instance of that emperor's predatory inclusion of artworks, buildings, and ultimately of large swathes of the city within his private palace. Just as light is made prisoner within the new, peculiar stone, the temple itself has also fallen victim to Nero's appetite, as well as to the uncontrolled growth of his house. Thanks to the example of the otherwise-unknown shrine at Cyzicus, Pliny clarifies that his harsh criticism of gold in interior decoration is limited to the private sphere. Significantly, the architect who had designed the building in Cyzicus and the sculptor who within the shrine dedicated an ivory statue of Jupiter with a marble Apollo crowning him—beautifully enlivened by the golden light emanating from the walls—were the same person. The result of his work was a *Gesamtkunstwerk* that could at once broadcast its maker's ingenuity (*ingenium*) and the use of prestigious materials (*materia*), chiefly *because* the latter remains cleverly concealed. The success of this project rests on the choice to exploit the physical properties of gold alone, such as colour and brilliance, instead of foregrounding its monetary value. As expected, the paradigm for the correct use of natural materials belongs to the religious sphere and the distant past, as opposed to the decadent private practices of Pliny's present. Here, Pliny explores the potential of sensual perception and experience in substantiating some of his fundamental lines of reasoning, binding the many streams of his work into one consistent argument about Nature and Man.

Notes

1 For an introduction to Pliny's final book, see Pérez González 2019; Voelke-Viscardi 2001; G. Rosati in Pliny-Conte 1982–1988, V, 743–745. In addition to the most widespread editions and translations, see Lefons 2000.

2 On the concept of *decor/decorum*, see Perry 2005, 28–64; Anguissola 2012, esp. 133–135.
3 Lao 2016, 223. On the introductions and conclusions of Pliny's books, see Naas 2002, 212–224.
4 In *Nat.* 37.80, Pliny comments upon the difficulty of describing gemstones.
5 The language employed in *Nat.* 37.1 (*coacta, contemplatio*) is similar to that used in Book 36, where Pliny addresses the idea of collecting by discussing the urban landscape of Rome (*Nat.* 36.27, 101, examined in Chapter 6). According to Platt 2018a, 229, Pliny's "holistic model of 'contemplation' [...] focuses less on classificatory hierarchies and divisions, and more on the interrelatedness of the system as a whole".
6 See *Nat.* 37.79, 83, 98, 112, 117, 119, 128, as well as *Nat.* 37.197–200, which concerns how to detect fake stones. Pliny discusses the forgery of coins in *Nat.* 33.132. For references to glass to detail the characteristics of less common substances, see *Nat.* 37.141, 149, 156.
7 Pliny describes the experience of viewing obsidian plaques. Unlike silver mirrors (*Nat.* 33.128–130), obsidian slabs placed on the walls reflect shadows instead of clear images (*Nat.* 36.196). On the Roman fascination with transparent and opaque materials in wall decorations, see Jones 2019, 137–178; Dubois-Pelerin 2008. The best-preserved first-century CE context for the display of obsidian 'mirrors' is the House of the Golden Cupids in Pompeii (VI 16, 7.38), discussed by Powers 2011, 17–19; McFerrin 2019.
8 Fire functions, according to Pliny, as an instrument for detecting falsifications (*Nat.* 37.200) and as a trigger for certain properties of gems (e.g., *Nat.* 37.51, 148).
9 *Nat.* 36.198 and 37.29. For the relationship between glass and rock crystal, see Crowley 2016, 229–231. Pliny's treatment of gems begins in earnest in *Nat.* 37.54, after presenting 'myrrhine' vases, rock crystal, and amber.
10 *Nat.* 37.204: rock crystal was found on the surface of the earth, while 'myrrhine' was mined.
11 On Pliny's account of 'myrrhine', see Tressaud and Vickers 2007; Butini 2019. On rock crystal in the Roman world, see Crowley 2016 and 2020.
12 Theophrastus (*On Stones* 11) describes the desiccating effect of the sun on formerly liquid substances.
13 *Nat.* 20.1, 24.1–3, 28.84, 37.59. Certain gems are said to either attract or repel other substances (*Nat.* 37.48, 61, 103–104, 147). On the concept of sympathy, see Schliesser 2015; Lehoux 2012, 122, 130–133; Gaillard-Seux 2003. Significantly, Pliny is the sole Latin source to use the Greek calque *antipathia*, thus demonstrating his keen interest in this concept and its precise articulation (index to Book 32; *Nat.* 20.1; 20.28; 24.67; 32.25; 34.150; 37.59).
14 *Nat.* 37.21, 23, 35, 42, 46, 75, 164. Theophrastus (*On Stones* 2–3) also discusses the creation of gems as a process revolving around solidification; see Caley and Richards 1956, 63–65.
15 Seneca, too, discusses the formation of rock crystal in his *Natural Questions* (3.25.12), see Crowley 2016, 221, 224; 2020, 152. On the tradition about the origins of rock crystal, see Buettner 2020, 118–121.
16 For Posidippus' poem, see Petrain 2005, 332–340; Belloni 2016. For an introduction to the *lithika*, see Acosta-Hughes, Kosmetatou, and Baumbach 2004; Gutzwiller 2005; Elsner 2014.

17 Transl. by David Petrain (2005, 332). For Posidippus' presentation of the rolling piece of rock crystal as an entirely natural object, see also Belloni 2016, esp. 8–9.
18 On Claudian's poetics within the framework of ancient paradoxography, see Guipponi-Gineste 2010, 266–279 and 2011; Harich-Schwarzbauer 2009, 24–27.
19 *Epigram* 33: *naturae signa prioris*. See comments in Crowley 2016, 240–241.
20 *Nat.* 37.96, 100, 132, 134, 182 (stars); 37.181 (moon); 37.100, 189 (flames).
21 *Nat.* 37.69, 110, 131, 133, 149, 155, 168, 171. Regarding the persistent association of gemstones and eyes in Roman thought, see Allen 2019.
22 See *Nat.* 37.184, 187, 188. For an example of 'imperfect solidification', see also *Nat.* 37.75. Occasionally, Pliny refers to gems as containing the *images* of animals and things: 37.5, 71, 179.
23 Introducing examples of miniature artworks (*Nat.* 7.85, 34.83, 36.43), Pliny again resorts to a comparison between small-scale objects and insects. On Theodorus' miniature chariot, see also Posidippus' epigram 67 AB, discussed by Kosmetatou 2004.
24 On bees and wax in Pliny's discourse on natural matters, see Platt 2020a.
25 On the terms *aequari* and *aequalis*, see Anguissola 2006, as well as Chapter 3 of this book.
26 *Nat.* 37.26, 56, 137 (hexagon); *Nat.* 37.144, 147 (cube); *Nat.* 37.176 (sphere); *Nat.* 37.105, 159 (heart). In *Nat.* 37.178, Pliny mentions a stone similar to crystal but with a greater number of facets. Elsewhere in Book 37, he mentions stones carved into regular prisms by skilled craftsmen (*Nat.* 37.76, 78–79). On the morphology of rock crystal according to the ancient written sources, see Crowley 2016, 222–223 and 2020, 154–155; Buettner 2020, 124–128.
27 For stones too delicate to be engraved, see *Nat.* 37.101, 120, 158 (on the contrary, amethysts are said to be easy to engrave in *Nat.* 37.121). In *Nat.* 37.8, Pliny introduces a historical perspective, noting that, in ancient times, gemstones would not have been engraved.
28 See Ballestrazzi 2020. Occasionally, Pliny mentions the process of ageing for gems (*Nat.* 37.70–71, 109, 134), which somehow binds these 'timeless' materials into the sphere of human experience.
29 See, also, *Nat.* 37.64 on the choice not to engrave emeralds, related to their use as lenses.
30 Pliny cuts short this list at *Nat.* 37.195, explaining that it is ultimately impossible to account for the endless (*innumera*) names given to different varieties of gems by his Greek sources.
31 In addition to the commonplace parallel with water and the sea, see *Nat.* 37.22, 26, 89, 136–137 (rainbow); 47, 121–122, 129, 150 (wine and grapes); 58, 77, 146, 147, 170 (metals); 63, 156, 180–181 (plants and grass); 72, 155 (feathers of birds); 102 (olive oil); 102, 170 (fruits); 113, 165 (vegetables or their juice); 114, 116, 122 (flowers); 115, 129 (sky); 128, 181–182 (honey); 142 (a lion's skin); 161 (shells); 162, 165, 169, 175 (blood); 171 (fish); 171 (earth); 181 (meat); and 185 (marble). A section of Book 37 (*Nat.* 37.186–192) is dedicated to gems organised according to their similarity—presumably in matters of colour—to parts of the body, animals, and inanimate objects. For Pliny's use of comparisons to account for the colour of gems, see Voelke-Viscardi 2001, 116–118. On the definition and symbolism of colour in Roman antiquity, see Romano 2003; Naas 2006; Bradley 2009, 87–110 in reference to Pliny's treatise.

32 Pliny invokes the similarity with emeralds for other materials: *Nat.* 37.84, 112, 115, 116, 118, 172.
33 Transl. from Shields 2016, 35. See also Thibodeau 2016, 135.
34 According to Claudius Ptolemy's second-century CE treatise on optics, all the "media that do not [completely] block the [visual ray's] passage" share the quality of transparency (*Optics* 5.1, transl. from Smith 1996, 229). On the concept of transparency, see Crowley 2016, 225–229; see also Voelke-Viscardi 2001, 120–121 for the place of this notion in Pliny's final book.
35 On geometry and reflection, see Plantzos 1997; Thibodeau 2016, 140–142. Interest in the properties associated with geometrical shapes emerges in the case of stones carved into multifaceted Euclidean solids, such as a highly polished icosahedron made of rock crystal, found in Rome, now at the Antikensammlung in Berlin (inv. 30891ss), see Platz-Horster 2012, 58 no. 12. A similar piece is in the National Archaeological Museum in Arezzo, see Crowley 2020, 154 fig. 1. For a discussion of Euclidean solids in Roman thought and visual culture, see Artmann 1993 and 1996.
36 Pliny also comments on the link between shape and reflection with regard to silver mirrors (*Nat.* 33.129).
37 For ancient sources on emeralds, see Plantzos 1997, 460–463.
38 Pliny's 'sensual' approach exemplifies what Porter 2011, 272 has defined an "aesthetic materialism", which is typical of the Hellenistic and Roman periods and their "object-oriented" sensibilities. On the "synaesthetic sensory economy" of ancient visual culture, see also Platt and Squire 2017, 104.
39 Bradley 2013, 140 comments that "the ancient colour experience could tap into smell, touch, taste and even sound. For Greeks and Romans, colour was a basic unit of perception".
40 For the likely identification of 'hyacinthus' with sapphire, see Pliny-Eichholz 1962, 266 note (a).
41 Looking at Indian agates, which remind viewers of rivers and woods, is considered good for the eyes (*Nat.* 37.40). See also *Nat.* 37.69, 129, 167 (as well as *Nat.* 37.101 for a stone capable of weakening sight).
42 See Plantzos 1997, 460–461.
43 Theophrastus refers to people carrying seals made of emerald to improve their sight by looking *at* them (*On Stones* 24). In *Nat.* 37.63 (cf. *Nat.* 29.132), Pliny reports that gem engravers used to refresh their eyes by resting them on the green surface of an emerald. In the following paragraph, he mentions an anecdote about emperor Nero, who allegedly used an emerald as a lens to watch the fight between gladiators, that is, looking *through* the stone (*Nat.* 37.64). Pliny's reliability on this information has been questioned by scholars who believe that the anecdote may be based on hearsay about Nero's poor eyesight (*Nat.* 11.144) and about his alleged habit of watching the games through small openings while reclining on a couch (Suetonius, *Nero* 12.2), see Woods 2006; Healy 1999, 241–245; Krug 1987.
44 For the concept of 'vibrant matter', see Barrett 2009.
45 Manolaraki 2018, 209, 222. Rosati 1997 highlights the Roman hostility towards perfumes as a symbol of decadence and the preference for an 'absence of smell'. On this perspective, Pliny's insistence on the scent of gems is all the more relevant for characterising his sensual criteria.
46 *Nat.* 37.64, 72, 95, 123 (viewing from specific angles); 37.127, 198 (viewing at certain points in the day).

47 This argument has been explored by Krug 1987, 470–471 with regard to two rings, which are now part of the collection of the Antikensammlung in Berlin (Platz-Horster 2012, 44–45 and 41 Fig. 8 no. E4).
48 *Nat.* 37.63, 66, 83, 101, 122, 131–133. On emeralds and their property of irradiating colour, see Theophrastus, *On Stones* 4, 23 (Caley and Richards 1956, 66–67, 98–99). For magnets, endowed by Nature with hands and the senses (*sensus manusque tribuit illi*), see *Nat.* 36.126.
49 Pliny's account of the temple in Cyzicus (on which, see Naas 2002, 370–371) finds no parallel in the ancient literary sources. Nonetheless, sacred buildings with translucent roofing, composed of thin marble slabs that let the daylight 'trickle down', are a well-known phenomenon in certain parts of the Greek world, see Ohnesorg 1993 and 2011; Heile 1990, esp. 27–28; Hoepfner 2001.
50 A. Corso in Pliny-Conte 1982–1988, V, 701; A. Rouveret in Pliny-André, Bloch, Rouveret 1981, 225.

2   Art and ethics

Plurima ex omnibus signa fecit, ut diximus, fecundissimae artis, inter quae destringentem se, quem M. Agrippa ante Thermas suas dicavit, mire gratum Tiberio principi. Non quivit temperare sibi in eo, quamquam imperiosus sui inter initia principatus, transtulitque in cubiculum alio signo substituto, cum quidem tanta pop. R. contumacia fuit, ut theatri clamoribus reponi apoxyomenon flagitaverit princepsque, quamquam adamatum, reposuerit.

(Natural History 34.62)

Pliny opens his presentation of Lysippus, a sculptor of bronze whom Alexander the Great chose as his official portraitist along with the painter Apelles (*Nat.* 7.125), by situating the master within (or, rather, *outside* of) the tradition of classical art, then proceeding to enumerate his most significant achievements. This section mentions the statue of an athlete using a body-scraper (in Greek, *Apoxyomenos*), which daringly depicts a three-dimensional figure of a youth with Lysippus' characteristic set of proportions (a relatively small head and slender body, *Nat.* 34.65) (Figure 2.1). In Pliny's account, such was Tiberius's fondness for the *Apoxyomenos* (*mire gratum* [...] *adamatum*) that he had the statue instated in his bedchamber (*in cubiculum*), putting another one in its place (*alio signo substituto*) at the Baths of Agrippa in the Campus Martius (although, owing to public pressure, the original would eventually be returned to its former location).[1]

Tiberius, whom the *Natural History* casts in a rather unfavourable light, was unable to resist his overwhelming passion for the statue, consistent with a pattern of behaviour that is commonly documented in the sources regarding this emperor.[2] Notwithstanding the somewhat gossipy dimension of this and similar anecdotes, it seems relevant to consider Pliny's choice of words and concepts for constructing the

DOI: 10.4324/9780429329159-2

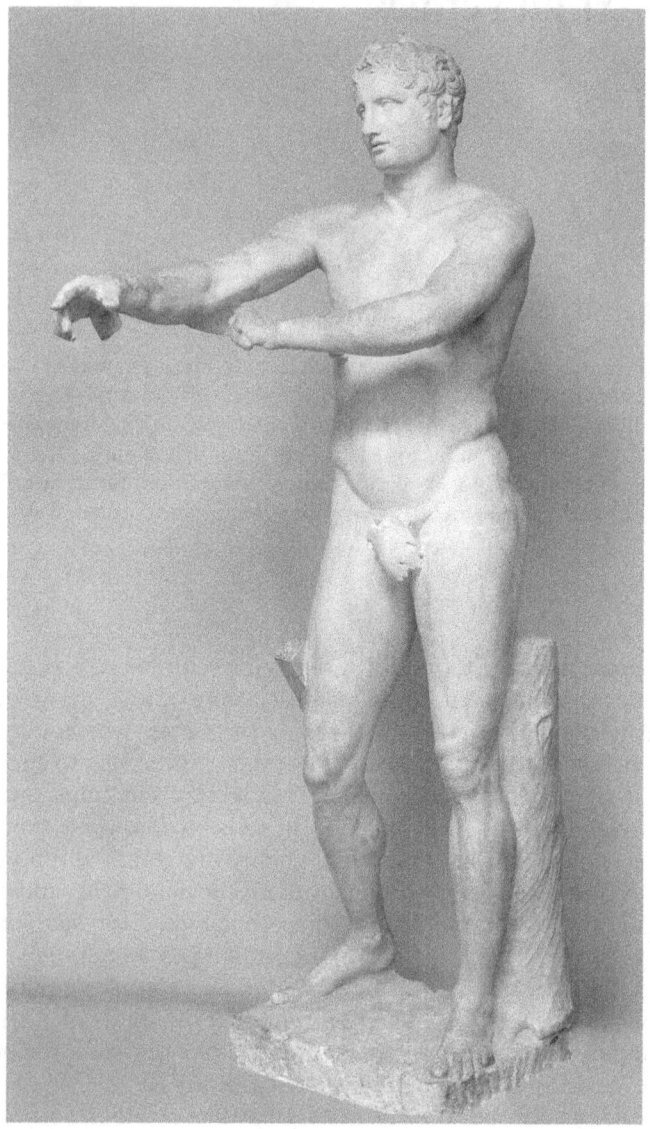

Figure 2.1 Statue of a man using the body-scraper (*Apoxyomenos*), considered to be a mid-first century CE replica of a fourth-century BCE
bronze original by Lysippus. Marble. H 205 cm. Vatican Museums, Museo Pio-Clementino, inv. no. 1185.

Credit: Rome, German Archaeological Institute (D-DAI-ROM-57.898, R. Sansaini).

character of public figures from the recent past through their artistic proclivities. In the *Natural History*, Tiberius' relationship with art is presented as one of indulgence and ruthless appropriation (*Nat.* 34.62 and 35.70). The artworks that he was fervent about (*adamatum, amavit*) were physically removed from the public sphere, and brought to (*transtulit*) and locked inside (*inclusit*) the most private of his palace's spaces: his bedchamber (*cubiculum*).

One cannot fail to notice the similarities in content and language with the presentation of another statue by Lysippus, the bronze statue of *Alexander the Great as a Boy*, which Pliny discusses immediately following his exposition of the *Apoxyomenos* (*Nat.* 34.63).[3] The portrait of Alexander had also fallen victim to the appetites of a reckless emperor. On Pliny's account, in a foolish attempt to increase the work's monetary value (*pretium*), Nero ordered that it be gilded (*inaurari*), thereby compromising its charm (*gratia artis*).[4] Although its gilded layer was eventually removed, Lysippus' bronze statue remained forever scarred. Pliny attributes the decision to disguise Lysippus' bronze surface under a coat of gold to Nero's infatuation with the artwork (*delectatus admodum*).[5] After all, Nero too was known for his inappropriate fascination with certain statues, which caused him to crave physical proximity to them.[6]

These two passages about Lysippus in Book 34 have in common certain critical details regarding the fraught relationship with art on the part of 'problematic' figures of the recent Roman past. In both cases, we are confronted with manipulations aimed at curtailing an object's network of contextual relationships, including other elements of its display and even the original artistic choices of its makers that were reflected in the work's material and surface qualities. With the artwork replaced in its location by another, the original system of relations is substituted with other, strictly personal interactions, especially those of the emperor, his private spaces, intimate desires, and political imagery. In this sense, the passages dedicated to Lysippus' *Apoxyomenos* and *Alexander as a Boy* give us occasion to explore the biographical potential of objects within Pliny's historical discourse. Thus, what role do material and social biographies of so-called 'embodied objects' play in determining their cultural significance and place within the narrative regarding Nature and the Roman empire?

Degrees of appropriation

Pliny presents the anecdote about Lysippus' *Apoxyomenos* as the paramount example of an illegitimate use of art, transferred from the domain of collective utility to one man's *cubiculum*, an intimate space for self-indulgent pleasure.[7] From this perspective, the appropriation of art and its removal from the public sphere reflects the prevailing patterns of behaviour in contemporary Roman society, ruled as it was by man's insatiable avidity for (*avaritia*), and unrestricted consumption of (*luxuria*), natural resources.

The abuse of art constitutes a leitmotif in Pliny's criticism of historical emperors. The discourse about art creates a conspicuous hierarchy comprising different levels of perversion that culminates with Nero.[8] Emperor Nero, together with Caligula, are figureheads around whom Pliny's narrative of corruption and immorality unfolds in contrast with the reinstated mores of Flavian Rome. Clearly, Nero's destructive attitude posed a much greater threat to the integrity of an artwork than Tiberius' merely foolhardy egoism. While Tiberius' transgressions were limited to the removal of artworks from public spaces, Nero's fervour extended to the point of altering artworks' material identity. Being incapable of recognising an artwork's value (albeit styling himself as an artist), the emperor naively believed that value coincided with material worth and gleaming surfaces.

Nero failed to recognise the role of both natural properties (such as the physical qualities of bronze) and technical skill (*ars*) in viewing and understanding art. Similarly, he thought that even a landmark of the city of Rome, such as Pompey's theatre, would require a covering of gold in the event of important ceremonies.[9] As indicated both by a passage regarding the gilding of a marble statue (*Nat.* 36.28) and another about the application of silver layers with figural motifs on bronze shields (*Nat.* 35.4), the practice of covering original sculptural surfaces with metal veneers was thought to weaken conspicuous details, thereby obscuring the hand (*manus*) of the maker.[10] The story of Nero's modification of the bronze portrait of Alexander may, of course, further hint at a more pointed political critique. This emperor's *imitatio Alexandri* may have raised a few eyebrows among his contemporaries, as well as his ambiguous divine assimilation, which was epitomised in Zenodorus' colossal (and very likely gilded) image of Nero as the god Helios.[11]

Although Tiberius is said to have been able to exercise some level of self-discipline, at least at the beginning of his principate (*imperiosus sui inter initia principatus*), the trajectory of both emperors is strikingly similar. This is especially true with regard to their increasing loss of control (*non quivit temperare sibi in eo*).[12] In particular, Pliny progressively constructs Nero's character through his misuse of natural substances: beginning with relatively harmless displays of wanton recklessness, to infliction of permanent damage which, as yet, did not annihilate the object, all the way to wholesale and irreversible destruction.[13] The *Natural History* depicts Nero (*Nat.* 37.29) at the very end of his reign—and in the very last book of the encyclopaedia—smashing two precious crystal vessels in a narcissistic outburst, having received a message that all was lost, thereby making "it impossible for any other man to drink from these cups".

We can situate this anecdote within a broader discourse regarding Nero's downfall, which relied on depictions of the emperor's engagement with the things around him in order to convey the despair and turmoil of the moment. According to Suetonius' narrative (sources for which may include Pliny's encyclopaedia),[14] the dismal news catches the emperor off guard as he is dining (*Nero* 47.1). Enraged, Nero tears to pieces the dispatches that have been handed to him and destroys his two favourite drinking cups (*duos scyphos gratissimi usus*) engraved with scenes from Homeric poetry. As others have previously observed, the relationship between the passages by Pliny and Suetonius is unclear, as is the material identity of Suetonius' *scyphi*. The section of Pliny's book on gems and precious stones, which immediately precedes the story of Nero's drinking vessels (*Nat.* 37.28), explains that only imperfect crystals marred by thin creases were engraved, which served to conceal their flaws (*artifices caelatura occultant*). Unblemished pieces (*sine vitio*), by contrast, required no *artifex* other than Nature herself and were therefore left untouched (*pura*). It is, of course, very possible that the two versions of Nero's end did in fact refer to different (whether real or fictional) objects (Figure 2.2).[15] However, other, more intriguing possibilities emerge when reading the sources with respect to one another. Is it possible that Nero's prized possessions may not be *intrinsically* that precious after all, their flaws being hidden under an artful lacework of engraved figures? Or might it be the case that the emperor, incapable of recognising Nature's perfection (just as he had misjudged the value of Lysippus' bronze), permitted the engraving of two flawless pieces of crystal *as if* this would up their value?

The brutality of Nero's final act is emphasised by the physical qualities of the material.[16] In the concluding book of the encyclopaedia, the presentation of rock crystal revolves around its peculiarity insofar as it is a perfect product of Nature, which does not require—and indeed surpasses—the work of any craftsman (37.26 and 28). Unsurprisingly, the consummate work of Nature cannot be successfully modified by man. Once it is broken, rock crystal "cannot be mended by any method whatsoever".[17] While the statue of *Alexander as a Boy*—composed by the best of bronze sculptors—emerged from its abuses worse off in

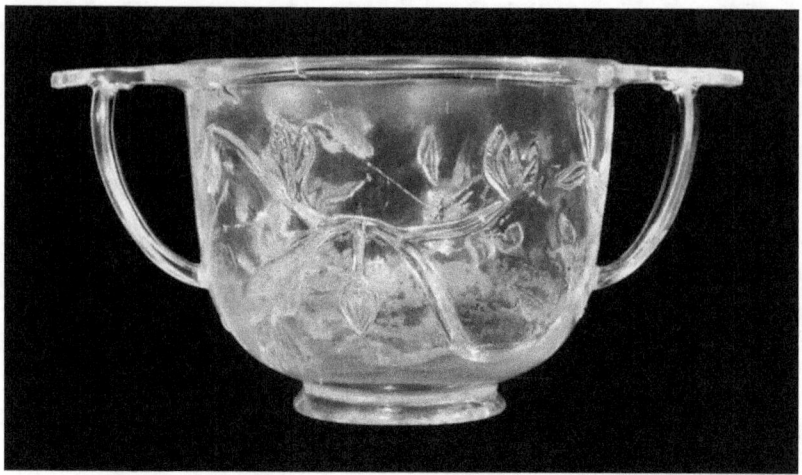

Figure 2.2 Cup (*skyphos*) from Santa Maria Capua Vetere, Augustan period. Rock crystal. H 12 cm. Naples, Museo Archeologico Nazionale, inv. no. 124701.

Credit: Naples, Museo Archeologico Nazionale.

terms of its *gratia artis*, it nonetheless clung to its celebrity. The same cannot be said of Nature's products, whose *gratia* no craftsman's *ars* can restore.

Layers of truth

It is clear from the story about Lysippus' portrait of Alexander that the quality and integrity of surfaces occupied a central place within Pliny's rhetoric regarding art, ingenuity, and propriety. Surfaces can either expose or disguise the material truth of an object, consequently revealing its position within the natural ranking of substances. Nero's order that the Alexander *puer* by Lysippus be gilded, while increasing (temporarily) the economic value of the statue, nonetheless concealed its artistic merit (*gratia*).[18] The problem here regards the intrinsic conflict between different elements of value—physical and sensory qualities, function, history, artistic merit, and price. This is especially true of gold, the substance that, above all others, had the power to rouse Nero's immoderate appetite (and Caligula's before him).[19] Being the substance that is itself used to determine other materials' commercial value (*Nat.* 33.1), the taste for gold expresses an aesthetic choice that privileges financial concerns over artistic merit.[20] Such is the impact of gold's monetary value that fervour towards the bare mineral has overtaken any admiration for the technical skill involved in its associated craft.

A further, more subtle layer of criticism applies to the practice of gilding, i.e., of concealing other substances under a thin layer of gold.[21] In Pliny's view, gilding falls under the category of 'compounds', which constitutes an inherently questionable classification.[22] The production of a compound is in itself considered to be an extravagant display of luxury, since it entails the manipulation of the products of Nature, which are in themselves perfect. The ideological dimension of the antithesis between (deceptive) *ars* and (genuine) *natura* is especially apparent in the types and uses of wood. In this field, extravagance takes the form of a reprehensible taste for veneer (*alia integi*), that is, the deceitful act of "making an outside skin for a cheaper wood out of a more expensive one" (*Nat.* 16.232–233).[23] Unsurprisingly, these artificial concoctions, which undermine the natural relationship between materials and value, allegedly had their heyday during the rule of Nero.[24] According to Pliny, at that time the taste for counterfeits even extended to the manufacture of wooden panels out of tortoiseshell— an egregious feat of deception. Rare and costly materials, the shells of tortoises were painted so as to shed any semblance of their authenticity (*ut pigmentis perderet se*), thereby imitating the ordinariness of wood, and embracing strategies of illusion that were both visual and intellectual.[25] Wood, which had come to be seen as second rate owing to its availability, was back in vogue as a fabrication (*modo luxuria non fuerat contenta ligno, iam lignum et e testudine facit*). A striking parallel for this remark is found in a passage devoted to silver vessels plated or inlaid with gold (*Nat.* 33.49), where this disingenous practice was presented as being so popular that gilded pieces had come to garner a higher price than those cast in solid gold.

Pliny's criticism of *inauratio* on decorative walls of private houses epitomises his argument regarding 'material deception' and its ethical corollaries. Consistent with Pliny's view about artistic development and social practices, questionable innovations (including the growing proclivity for covering interior walls with coats of marble and gold) coincide with the reign of Nero (*Nat.* 35.2–4). In the opening paragraphs of his book on pigments, Pliny bemoans the decline of painting, thereby castigating the coarsening taste of his contemporaries, who seem to be less interested in figural painting over simple, earnest plaster than they are in marble veneers, to the point that they even cover the latter in gold.[26] A passage from Book 33, which provides the starting point for the discussion in Chapter 4, details the lamentable evolution of this technique from the public (sacred) to the private sphere (*Nat.* 33.57). While the gilding of inner environments and statues appears to be a permissible practice in the sacred sphere and is, more importantly, traditional, its use as a means for emphasising private ownership and dominion over Nature emerges as a testament to moral corruption. In light of this discussion, it is clear that passages about gilding are essential to Pliny's denunciation of the perverse ideology behind the technological progress of his time, which rested on a taste for deception and illusoriness rather than a straightforward appreciation of Nature's truth.

Traces for memory

The unstable, tenuous border between human ingenuity and impudence reflects a conflict that is inherent in Pliny's understanding of political expansion and economic growth. This intrinsic contradiction is made explicit in a passage from the Book 24 on medical botany (*Nat.* 24.4–5). There, Pliny complains that "compound prescriptions and mysterious mixtures" (*compositiones et mixturae inexplicabiles*) from ingredients extracted in remote countries have replaced traditional wisdom and humble herbs, which are "easy to discover and cost nothing". Rome's hegemony over a vast empire permitted access to information and resources that were ultimately the *raison d'être* of, and rationale for, Pliny's encyclopaedia. However, the availability of new substances and practices posed a vital threat to the survival of ancient traditions, which society increasingly saw as obsolete.

The criticism of gold, gilding, and of deceptive compounds in general has its roots in Pliny's sweeping denunciation of the moral decline that constitutes the inherent disadvantage of Roman expansion. In accounting for the practices discussed in this chapter, the problem ultimately materialises as one of *memory* or, more pointedly, *loss* and *forgetting*. This passage into mnemonic oblivion takes the form of forgetfulness about material identities, such as the painted shells of tortoises that lose the guise of authenticity, *perderet se* (*Nat.* 16.233); the names of those who worked with lavish gold rather than engaging in the "formerly illustrious" art of painting (*Nat.* 35.2);[27] and the craftsman's hand (*manus*), thanks to the gilding of his creation (*Nat.* 36.28).[28] In severing the *physical* connections between the two, original agents of a given object (Nature, as the maker of all substances, and the human artisan, who forms man-made products), the act of veneering is adduced for populating the Roman world with disconnected, 'anonymous' artefacts, absent of genealogical relations and, therefore, *inexplicable*.

Anecdotes regarding Lysippus' bronzes, which had been appropriated and adulterated by reckless emperors, provide excellent cases for unpacking Pliny's complex relationship with the concept of memory. Pliny dwells on the consequences of both of these incidents, and the role that public opinion played in reversing the emperors' imprudent decisions. Such was the public outcry, imploring Tiberius to return (*reponi*) the *Apoxyomenos* to its location in the Baths of Agrippa, that the emperor had no choice but to agree (*reposuerit*). Here, the repetition of the verb *reponere* ('to put back', 'to restore') captures the rapidity of the exchange and Tiberius' ultimate deference to the people's demands.[29]

In the case of Lysippus' portrait of Alexander, it was the choice to remove the golden layer (likely after the emperor's demise) that actually ended up *increasing* the value of the statue (*pretiosiorque talis existimabatur*), even if—or rather *because*—its surface was beset with scars and incisions. In other words, in the case of a centuries-old masterpiece, the addition of an expensive material does little to enhance the work's overall significance, which rather benefits from a sort of 'biographical patina'. This discussion of fame as a product of visible flaws on the artwork's surface bears very close similarities to the story (*Nat.* 35.91) of Apelles' famous painting of Aphrodite 'rising from the sea' (*Anadyomene*), which I discuss in Chapter 5. According to Pliny, this picture was greatly admired owing to its signs of age (*iniuria*), although it had also fallen victim to Nero's maladroit conduct.

Clearly, in the case of *Alexander as a Boy*, the performative traces of Nero's offence, and of its removal, added to the statue's significance, rendering it an effective mnemonic of both imperial abuse and, more broadly, the consequences of artworks' illegitimate usage.[30] It is, after all, through this inherent tension between *forgetting* and *reminding*— or, more precisely, between *deleting* and *reminding*—that Pliny considers Nero's monumental and artistic heritage in light of the Flavian political program and propaganda. While the meaning of Nero's most famous gilded artwork (his own colossal image displayed in the vestibule of the *Domus Aurea*) was 'corrected' by essentially renaming the figure, which Vespasian had changed into an image of the Sun (*Nat.* 34.45),[31] in order for the statue of Alexander to be removed from the shadow of the disgraced emperor, it was necessary to restore its material identity. A new interpretation of Nero's colossus could be provided simply by playing on the statue's original *double entendre*, which referred to both an emperor and a god. However, in the case of Lysippus' *Alexander*, reminders of Nero's vandalism (and thereby of the emperor's moral corruption) were kept alive by the removal of its materiality and by directing attention to its vestiges.

It is difficult to escape the ways in which Pliny's narrative spotlights various visual strategies in the deliberate manipulation of memory.

With this, the Roman public were all too familiar. Indeed, the wide-spread practice of reworking portraits of disgraced emperors, which were defaced or turned into images of their successors, often left visible traces of the transformation. Examples of this from the *corpus* of Nero's portraits are numerous. The features of Nero, for instance, were transformed into those of Titus on an onyx cameo in Florence, depicting the emperor in the guise of Jupiter with an oak-leaf crown (*corona civica*), a sceptre straddled by an eagle, and an aegis over his shoulder (Figure 2.3).[32] However, at least the most careful spectators would still have been able to recognise Nero's characteristic coiffure, which creates "a kind of hybrid Nero-Titus configuration", thereby

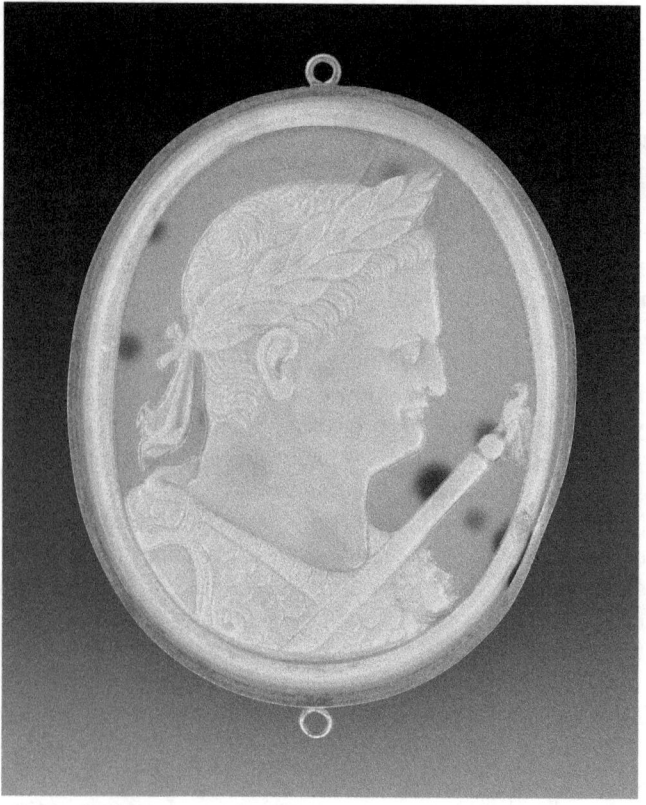

Figure 2.3 Onyx cameo with the portrait of Titus as Jupiter, possibly reworked from a portrait of Nero. 7.9 × 6.5 cm. Florence, Museo Archeologico Nazionale, inv. no. 14546.

Credit: Florence, Museo Archeologico Nazionale.

foregrounding the "transformative history" of the piece through the very act of erasing the former emperor's face.[33] In a similar way, the restoration of Lysippus' bronze surface was not intended to prevent the recollection of Nero's behaviour, but rather served to highlight the *conscious return* to a moment before his reign, as well as the *collective consensus* regarding this effort (since the piece's value did, in fact, increase following its restoration).

Notes

1 On the use of *substituere* in reference to actions of deceit and artistic incompetence, see Chapter 5.
2 For example, the painting of a high priest of Cybele (*Archigallus*) by Parrhasius (*Nat.* 35.70) that Tiberius loved dearly (*amavit*) and allegedly locked in his bedroom (*cubiculo suo inclusit*). Anecdotes about Tiberius' erotic misuses of art are by no means limited to the *Natural History* (see Suetonius, *Tiberius* 44.2). For the Latin sources' association of private displays of art and the concepts of *libido, voluptas, cupiditas, amor*, see Robert 2013, 240–242.
3 See Anguissola and Faedo (forthcoming), and Vout 2017, 181–183.
4 A later Greek source, a discourse by Julian the Apostate (2.4), includes a comparable anecdote about the marble statue of Eros at Thespiae, made by Praxiteles. Apparently, the decision to have its wings gilded reduced the accuracy of the artwork (τὴν ἀκρίβειαν ἀφελεῖν τῆς τέχνης). Significantly, this story is also the product of human *avaritia*: carried off to Rome by Caligula, the *Eros* was restored to its original location by Claudius and later removed again by Nero (Pausanias, *Description of Greece* 9.27.4). A misguided effort in reaching heightened visual effects is discussed also by Plutarch with regard to Domitian's interventions on the Capitoline temple (*Life of Publicola* 15.4) and the re-cutting of its columns (which gained little in smoothness, γλαφυρία, while losing in symmetry and beauty).
5 For Pliny's use of the word *delectatus* with regard to the appropriation and removal to Rome of either an artwork or a material, see *Nat.* 35.131 and 36.49.
6 In *Nat.* 34.82, Pliny mentions Nero's sensual love for the *Amazon* by Strongylion, the artist who also created Brutus' beloved *Boy*, see Isager 1991, 95; Pliny-Le Bonniec, Gallet de Santerre 1953, 81, 263.
7 On the *cubiculum* as a 'moral space' in Latin literature, see Riggsby 1997; Anguissola 2007b and 2010, 37–67. In *Nat.* 35.26, Pliny famously argues for moderation in the display of art, which should be accessible to the public rather than hidden away for the enjoyment of the few (see Chapter 6). Contrasts with the stance of the Flavian emperors are apparent in Pliny's narrative of Vespasian's restitution to the public of the many artworks looted by Nero, which populated his *Domus Aurea* (*Nat.* 34.84). See also Titus' behaviour, when he displayed the *astragalizontes* made by Polyclitus in the *atrium* of his *domus* (*Nat.* 34.55), a space accessible to visitors (Vitruvius, *On Architecture* 6.5 famously presents the *cava aedium* among

the domestic spaces *communia cum extraneis*, which could be entered even without invitation). The ambivalence of Pliny's moral judgement surfaces when he refrains from further commentary on the location of the artwork that he considers superior to anything else, the *Laocoon* group, displayed in an unspecified location *in Titi imperatoris domo* (*Nat.* 36.37).

8 For Pliny's attitude towards earlier Roman emperors, see Baldwin 1995; Naas 2002, 98–99. In the book on anthropology and human physiology (*Nat.* 7.45), Caligula and Nero are dismissed as "the two firebrands of mankind", and, immediately afterwards (in *Nat.* 7.46), Nero is once again mentioned as an "enemy of mankind". See also Pliny's criticism of Nero in *Nat.* 30.14–15.

9 *Nat.* 33.54. The Theatre of Pompey is presented in contrast to Nero's *Domus Aurea*, which was much larger and represented an incomparably more deplorable waste of resources, see La Rocca 2017a, 202.

10 In *Nat.* 35.4 Pliny explains that the practice of covering bronze shields with designs in silver produces only clumsy images (*surdo figurarum discrimine*, translated in Pliny-Rackham 1961, 263 as "with only a faint difference between the figures", in Pliny-Croisille 1985, 37 as "la distinction entre les traits individuels est ignorée", and by R. Mugellesi in Pliny-Conte 1982–1988, V, 297 as "senza alcuna sensibilità nel differenziare le figure"). In *Nat.* 36.28, Pliny discusses the effects of gilding on a statue of Janus Pater, which had effaced the hand of its maker.

11 On Nero's *imitatio Alexandri*, see Demandt 2009, 413, while on the relationship between gold and Nero's solar imagery, see Bergmann 2013, 342–351 and 1994, 5–6. For the colossus of Zenodorus, see also Albertson 2001; Ensoli 2002 and 2007, esp. 409–410, 416–417; Carey 2003, 156–165.

12 For Tiberius' alleged psychological evolution, see also *Nat.* 14.144.

13 Nero's destructive attitude finds a parallel in Caligula's act of vandalism against the wall paintings of *Helena* and *Atalanta* at Lanuvium (*Nat.* 35.17–18), which had ignited his lust (*libidine accensus*) to such an extent that he attempted to tear them off the wall (see Chapter 6). Another incident of 'desctructive passion' is in *Nat.* 37.18, where Pliny mentions an ex-consul who was so fond (*ob amorem*) of a myrrhine cup that he would gnaw its rim. The damage only increased the vessel's price (*ut tamen iniuria illa pretium augeret*), by making its material worth even more conspicuous. See also the story of Cleopatra's pointless destruction of two pearls on a bet (*Nat.* 9.120–121), as well as the similar instances of 'gastronomic destruction' of natural resources mentioned in *Nat.* 8.31.

14 See Sansone 1993, 187–188. On the biographies of Nero, see Hurley 2013 and Barton 1994. On the construction of Nero's character through the narrative about his dinner parties, see Schulz 2019, 11–32. The episode of Nero's cups finds an intriguing parallel in the story about Petronius' death (*Nat.* 37.20), who allegedly destroyed one of his precious possessions (a mytthine *trulla*, 'ladle') as an act of contempt towards Nero (*invidia Neronis*), "thereby depriving the Emperor's dining-room table of this legacy".

15 Sansone (1993, 188 note 36) believes the passages unrelated with regard to the identity of the vessels. The fascination with rock-crystal vessels and their imitations in Nero's times is also attested by *Nat.* 36.195.

16 This issue is all the more relevant to the investigation of the literary construction of Nero's character 'through his objects' if one recalls the famous anecdote about the so-called *Neronis decocta*. According to multiple sources (*Nat.* 31.40; Suetonius, *Nero* 48.3; Cassius Dio, *Roman History* 63.28.5), emperor Nero first discovered how to produce a pleasant, cold drink by boiling water, then cooling it by placing it in a glass vessel and plunging it into the snow. Whereas Pliny presents this as an act of *voluptas*, Wood 2009 situates Nero's discovery within a prevailing proclivity for cold remedies. Regarding the vessel supposedly used by Nero for his *decocta*, it may be useful to refer to what Pliny says about crystal being used for cold drinks only (*Nat.* 37.26 and 30).

17 The story about Nero's cups belongs to a small set of anecdotes about the deliberate destruction of non-restorable items and the sense of sorrow for their loss (e.g., *Nat.* 37.19), see Isager 1991, 215–216. On the brittleness of crystal and its moral implications, see also *Nat.* 33.5. In *Nat.* 37.19 Pliny mentions having seen the fragments (*unius scyphi fracti membra*) of a broken myrrhine cup displayed to the public "as a sign of the sorrows of the age and the ill-will of Fortune".

18 In Lucian's parodic dialogue *Iuppiter Tragoedus* (*Zeus Rants* 7–12), the Greek gods discuss the criteria for assigning a place in council to each of them, that is, to their sculptural representation. Although ranking in accordance with material seems quite straightforward at first, it raises three questions. First, is a statue of solid gold intrinsically superior to finer creations in bronze or marble? Second, is the material more important than the subject represented? Third, does material count more than its quantity (i.e., is a gold statuette worthier than a bronze colossus)? Lucian's dialogue, of course, is different from Pliny's encyclopaedia in many respects. Nevertheless, both seem to mirror an ongoing discourse regarding the relative merits of materials and craftsmanship, as well as the long philosophical debate about causality.

19 On Caligula, *avidissimus auri*, see *Nat.* 33.79.

20 For a commentary on *Nat.* 33.1–3, see Zehnacker 1983.

21 Pliny introduces the techniques for gilding in *Nat.* 33.64–65, 100, 125. The literature on gilding in ancient art is discussed in Faedo 2020. In *Nat.* 34.15, Pliny presents the practice of gilding bronze statues (*auro integere*) as a relatively recent invention, for "it certainly has a name of no long standing at Rome". According to Pliny-Le Bonniec, Gallet de Santerre 1953, 179, Pliny may refer here to the word *auratura*, which is first attested in the age of Augustus. On the introduction of gilded statues to Italy, see also Livy, *History of Rome* 40.34.1.

22 The criticism of compounds is clear in *Nat.* 9.139, 13.1, 13.17–18, 14.2–3, 14.130, 22.118, 24.4–5, 29.24–25, 33.49. This criticism culminates in the passages devoted to perfumes and pharmaceutical drugs, ingenious compounds that relied on expensive ingredients sent from the East and India. The best-known instance of this interest in unnatural compounds is Mithridates' *thēriakē*, with its 54 ingredients (*Nat.* 29.24–25, *excogitata compositio luxuriae*). For the passages on Eastern perfumes and Mithridates' anecdote, see Blonski 2007; Beagon 1992, 228–229; Jones-Lewis 2012, esp. 61–66. On Mithridates as an avid collector of various objects

and substances, see also *Nat.* 37.11. On Pliny's treatment of exotic *aromata* and substances especially from the commercial point of view, see Taborelli 1991 and 1994. In *Nat.* 11.61, Pliny hints that bees—animals to which he attributes extraordinary qualities of discipline and laboriousness—do not tolerate artificial odours and attack people who wear perfume.

23 For Pliny's criticism against cutting marble into slices (*secare luxuriaque dividere*) and covering the inner spaces of private houses with a marble layer (*Nat.* 33.57, 35.2–3, 36.48 and 51), see Chapter 4. See also *Nat.* 34.13 on the criticism of bronze veneers.

24 Nero's taste for compounds and veneers also emerges in *Nat.* 33.90, where Pliny reports that the emperor had "the sand of the circus sprinkled with gold-solder" (Reitzenstein 2016). See also *Nat.* 33.140 for the empress Poppaea's similar preferences, which involved having the hooves of her favourite mules gilded. Pliny again discusses the taste for shiny or colourful reflections on architectural materials with regard to the Circus Maximus in *Nat.* 36.162 (apparently, the *lapis specularis* had been used to decorate the building), see A. Corso in Pliny-Conte 1982–1988, V, 171.

25 In this passage, Pliny also complains about the practice of painting the horns of animals. See also *Nat.* 33.146.

26 See Pliny-Croisille 1985, 132–134 and A. Corso in Pliny-Conte 1982–1988, V, esp. the notes on pp. 293, 295, 297. Pliny criticises the gilding of wooden structures as an example of *luxuria* also in *Nat.* 36.114.

27 In *Nat.* 35.2, painting is said to be an *arte quondam nobili*, which could ennoble "others whom it deigned to transmit to posterity".

28 On this passage, which is about a marble statue of Janus that had been gilded, resulting in the impossibility of recognising its maker's hand, see Faedo 2020, as well as Anguissola and Faedo (forthcoming). Significantly, Pliny discusses the deceptive potential of gilding in relation to the art of Scopas, Praxiteles, and Lysippus, three late-Classical masters who had reached unprecedented heights in the portrayal of interiority and emotions. Together with the quality of surface treatment, polychromy counts among other surface values that gilding would suppress. It seems no coincidence that one of the putative creators of the marble statue of Janus, Praxiteles, famously submitted his best work to the painter Nicias for the *circumlitio*, a final touch of painting (*Nat.* 35.133). On *circumlitio*, see Malaspina 2020.

29 None of the most influential translations of Pliny's treatise reflects this element of the text: Pliny-Le Bonniec, Gallet de Santerre 1953, 129; Pliny-Rackham 1961, 175; Pliny-Jex-Blake, Sellers 1968, 51; Pliny-König, Bayer 1989, 51; R. Mugellesi in Pliny-Conte 1982–1988, V, 185; Pliny-Ferri 2000, 107.

30 I borrow the concept of 'performative traces' from a paper ('Periferie, epitomi, residui: strategie dell'attenzione') delivered by Salvatore Settis at the Kunsthistorisches Institut of Florence, as part of the symposium *Detail und Aufmerksamkeit* (May 2014).

31 On the relationship between gold and Nero's solar imagery, see Bergmann 2013, 342–351 and 1994, 5–6. On Nero's portraits with a radiate crown, see La Rocca 2017a, 197–202. I discuss the *Domus Aurea* as a '*locus*' of forgetting' in Chapter 6.

32 Florence, Museo Archeologico Nazionale, inv. no. 14546. See M.E. Micheli in Giuliano 1989, 246–247 no. 178; Megow 1993.

33 Quotations are from Varner 2017, 244. Varner discusses a comparable instance of defacement on a portrait of Nero (now in Cagliari, Museo Nazionale, inv. no. 6122), which, in addition to being damaged, had the word *VICTO* ("to the vanquished") incised on the breast (2004, 49–50, 237 cat. no. 2.1, fig. 42). A notable example of this meaningful use of 'performative traces' is the (much later) painted tondo from the Fayum (now in Berlin), which depicts the family of Septimius Severus (Antikensammlung, inv. no. 31329). There, the emperor's younger son Geta's facial features have been brutally erased following his murder at the hands of Caracalla. Nonetheless, his draped bust and the signs of his former imperial status—the sceptre and crown—have been just as carefully preserved, thereby drawing attention to the magnitude of the erasure, see Varner 2004, 181–182.

3 Art and language

Primus hic multiplicasse veritatem videtur, numerosior in arte quam Polyclitus et in symmetria diligentior, et ipse tamen corporum tenus curiosus animi sensus non expressisse, capillum quoque et pubem non emendatius fecisse, quam rudis antiquitas instituisset.

(*Natural History* 34.58)

The paragraphs dedicated to Polyclitus (*Nat.* 34.55–56) and Myron (*Nat.* 34.57–58), two celebrated fifth-century BCE sculptors of bronze, follow a similar structure. Both sections open by placing each master in the geographical (*Nat.* 34.55, 57) and artistic landscape (both pupils of Hagelades) of their time. A list of masterpieces follows, with one piece from each sculptor singled out for lengthier praise (Polyclitus' *Canon* and Myron's *bucula*, 'The Cow'). Concluding remarks set each artist's work in a broader perspective, relating learned opinion on his achievements and establishing an explicit comparison with the master discussed immediately before. Constructed around the familiar sequence of invention and improvement, this progression has roots in Greek thought and must have been deeply ingrained in Pliny's Hellenistic sources.[1]

Pliny acknowledges (*Nat.* 34.56) Polyclitus' contribution to perfecting and refining (*consummasse, erudisse*) the science (*scientiam*) of bronze sculpture, which was revealed by Phidias (*aperuisse*). Polyclitus is credited with the discovery of how to make statues throw "their weight on one leg" (*uno crure ut insisterent signa*). However (*tamen*), Varro reportedly objected that Polyclitus' figures were "almost all made on one model" (*paene ad exemplum*).[2] The discussion of Myron's art is constructed in explicit response to this, as Myron appears to have surpassed Polyclitus in two qualities: being *numerosus* ("rich in rhythms") and *diligens* in matter of *symmetria* ("assiduous in the pursuit of correct proportions"). Nonetheless (*tamen*), he too (*et ipse*) seemed little interested in the expression of feelings (*animi sensus non*

DOI: 10.4324/9780429329159-3

expressisse) and made no progress in the representation of details such as the hair. The first master who was thought to have rendered (*expressit*) the sinews, veins, and hair with some care (*diligentius*) is Pythagoras from Rhegium, mentioned immediately after Myron (*Nat.* 34.59).

The passage cited at the beginning of this chapter provides an exemplary case study to explore Pliny's language regarding the visual arts.[3] The *Natural History* draws on a large selection of sources and mirrors the choices, narrative strategies, tastes, and language of its (mostly Greek) predecessors, in addition to the author's own idiosyncrasies. The section from Book 34 devoted to the art of Myron fosters questions that are crucial for understanding Pliny's relationship to his sources and their theoretical framework. How does Pliny succeed in appropriating the technical language of individual disciplines, making it accessible to his readers and integrating it in the encyclopaedia as a whole? Do certain terms and the concepts they encapsulate hint at broader preoccupations about intellectual work and Pliny's own position as the provider of "an all-round education"? Finally, how does the idea of artistic competition play into the broader discourse on human progress?

The rhythm of symmetry

For scholars, the statement about Myron's art poses thorny challenges that emerge from discrepancies across its translation into modern languages. Myron's main contribution to the progress of sculpture seems to consist of the rather ambiguous accomplishment of having "multiplied truth" (*multiplicasse veritatem*).[4] One essential problem with understanding this comment is an apparent contradiction with other Latin accounts of the art of Myron, above all to Cicero's famous judgement of his statues as "not sufficiently life-like" (*Brutus* 70: *non satis ad veritatem adducta*), with the feature of *veritas* ('truth') being insufficiently attained.[5]

A possible explanation for the apparent inconsistency between Cicero's dialogue on oratory and Pliny's chapters on sculpture could lie in the two authors' different perspectives and, consequently, in their diverging views of *veritas* as an ingredient of artistic creation. In articulating a commonplace parallel between the evolution of rhetoric and the visual arts,[6] Cicero hints at a more generic progression towards naturalism. Pliny, instead, is interested in detailing the distinctive features of each master's production. As Silvio Ferri suggested almost 80 years ago, the key to understanding Pliny's verdict is likely found in the close analogy between the Greek and Latin languages of rhetoric and of art criticism.[7] As a technical term in the field of rhetoric, *multiplicatio* refers to a specific strategy to increase the impact of a concept by means

of repetition in slightly different forms.[8] In the treatise on oratory written by Quintilian in roughly the same period as Pliny's *Natural History*,
the method of *multiplicatio* is treated under the more general heading
of *amplificatio* (*Institutes of Oratory* 8.4.26–27), i.e., the "accumulation
of words and sentences with the same meaning". This definition is close
to the one Quintilian uses for the Greek notion of πλοκή, a *repetitio fre-
quentior* of certain concepts and clauses (*Institutes of Oratory* 9.3.41).[9]
In the sphere of the visual arts, the 'multiplication of truth' may also
refer to compositions based on the repetition of shapes and lines—that
is, of individual, measurable elements of naturalistic mimesis.[10]

According to Pliny, Myron surpassed Polyclitus in terms of his ability
to be more *numerosus* and more careful in matters of *symmetria*. Some
scholars have interpreted the word *numerosus* as 'prolific' or 'versatile'.
But in Pliny's sections on the visual arts, it seems to point instead to
an artist's reliance on *numeri* or forms and shapes with measurable
proportions.[11] Following this, a viable explanation emerges in light of
an analogy between the Latin word *numerus* and the Greek *rhythmos*
(ῥυθμός), which Latin technical literature on rhetoric explicitly discusses as synonymous.[12] When describing the importance of *rhythmos*
for organising discourse, Aristotle identified a fundamental distinction between metrical (ἔμμετρον) prose and prose lacking rhythm altogether (ἄρρυθμον): the former appears artificial and therefore not
entirely persuasive, while the latter sounds boundless and distracting.
The recommended form of diction is thus rhythmical (εὔρυθμον), constructed around a carefully balanced rhythmic sequence that is both
easy to grasp and natural in sound (*Rhetorics* 1408b–1409a).[13] In his
first-century BCE treatise on the oratory of Demosthenes, Dionysius
of Halicarnassus decries metrical prose (ἔμμετρον or ἔρρυθμον) as dan-
gerously akin to poetry and singing. Instead, he makes the case for
rhythmical (εὔρυθμον) discourse (*Demosthenes* 50).[14] Cicero elaborates
along the same line, stating that in spoken prose "a passage is regarded
as rhythmical (*numerosum*) not when it is composed entirely of metrical forms (*non quod totum constat e numeris*), but when it comes very
close to being so" (*Orator* 198). Prose without a rhythmical pattern
sounds "disordered, unpolished, and vague". But in rhythmical compositions (*numerosa oratio*) "the order of the words produces a rhythm
(*ordo enim verborum efficit numerum*) without any apparent effort on
the part of the orator" (*Orator* 219–220).[15] In his reference to Myron
as *numerosus*, Pliny may have employed similar critical categories to
those well established in the field of rhetoric and easy to grasp for his
contemporaries, who were accustomed to comparison between the
development of the visual arts and certain literary genres. His comments about Myron may have been intended to highlight the master's

'rhythmical' concept of visual mimesis based on repetition, juxtaposition, and emphasis of distinctive measurable elements. Myron's being *numerosus* would explain his relentless pursuit of *veritas*.

Along with the concepts of *numerus* (rhythm) and *numerosus* (rich in rhythms), *veritas* only appears in a handful of other passages in Pliny's final five books (*Nat.* 35.65, 103, 130).[16] In contrast, the encyclopaedia explores the meaning of *symmetria* (the commensurability of parts) more closely. At a later point in Book 34, Pliny states that Lysippus "scrupulously preserved" the quality of *symmetria*, "for which there is no word in Latin" (*Nat.* 34.65).[17] The notion of *symmetria* had occupied a central position in both Greek philosophy and discourse on the visual arts since the Classical period. According to Vitruvius (*On Architecture* 3.1.1), it coincides with the search for correct proportions (*proportio*, in Greek ἀναλογία). Proportions, in turn, consist of correspondence (*commodulatio*) between the individual parts of a work.[18] Famously commenting that the principles behind the design of a temple are ultimately identical to those determining the appearance of a well-shaped man (*uti hominis bene figurati*), Vitruvius highlights the fundamental equivalence of critical categories in the discussion of both architecture and human images. This shared idea of measurement was deeply ingrained in the Greek approach to making and viewing art, as evidenced in the case of metrological reliefs that represent the main measures of length using the parts of the human body.[19] Returning to the *Natural History*, Pliny appears keenly aware of the challenge that foreign (Greek) words may pose to his readers.[20] When possible, he provides both the foreign technical term and its Latin, often less specific counterpart.[21] In the case of a crucial concept such as *symmetria*, which lacks a fitting Latin adaptation, Pliny alerts his readers and implicitly addresses the suspicion that he may have researched his subject less than adequately.

When discussing the art of Myron, Pliny probably follows his Greek sources in resorting to terms and expressions peculiar to the language of oratory. Seen as highly proficient in the rhythmical construction of figures (*numerosus*) and careful in pursuit of mathematical harmony (*symmetria*), Myron would have suggested dynamism through the repetition and alternation of measurable segments (*multiplicare veritatem*). His characteristically 'fragmented composition' may have been the reason why Cicero, who uses the word *veritas* in its most widespread meaning as 'fidelity to nature', finds that Myron's statues do not quite succeed at a faithful imitation of reality. This line of thought also illuminates Quintilian's mention of one of Myron's best-known masterpieces, the *Discobolus* ('Discus-Thrower'), as "twisted and elaborate" (*distortum et elaboratum*) but nonetheless worthy of praise for the novelty and difficulty (*novitas ac difficultas*) of the artistic invention (*Institutes of Oratory* 2.13.10).[22] Latin literary sources share a fundamental appreciation for Myron's ingenuity, even as they voice their troubles accounting for Myron's 'rhythmically elaborate' compositions. The statue of the *Discobolus*, of which a large series of later Roman marble copies has survived (Figure 3.1), offers a relevant case

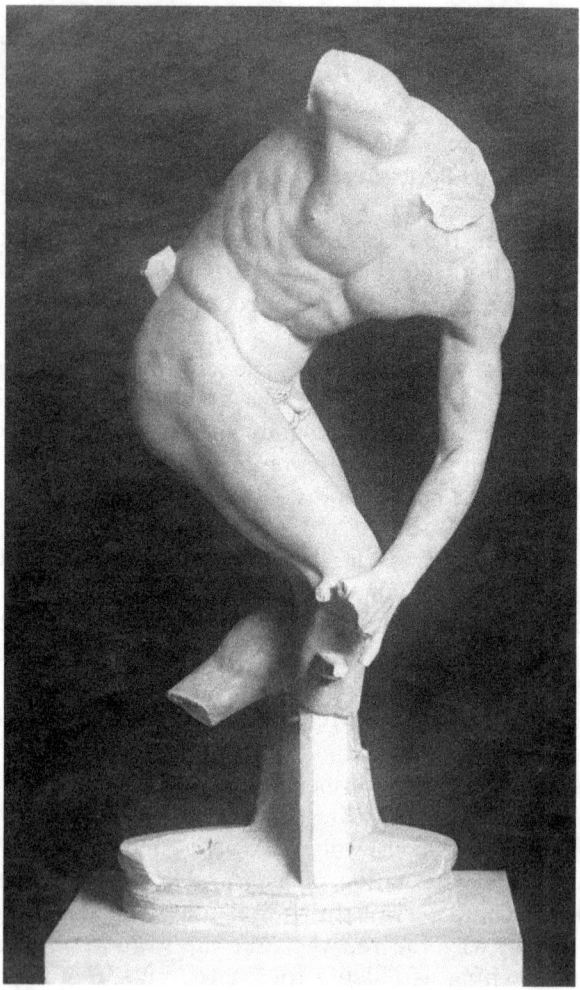

Figure 3.1 Statue of an athlete throwing the discus (*Discobolus*), considered a replica of a mid-fifth-century BCE bronze original by Myron. Marble. H 138 cm from the right shoulder to the upper side of the plinth. Rome, Museo Nazionale Romano, inv. no. 56039.

Credit: Rome, German Archaeological Institute (D-DAI-ROM-1706).

in point to address the ancient reception of Myron's art.[23] Much of the impact of this image lies in the artist's choice to break the figure down into a sequence of straight and curved lines, creating a momentuous tension between the expectation of rotatory, forward movement and the depicted present state of concentrated stability.

Degrees of precision

Lysippus, the trusted author of Alexander the Great's sculptural portraits, preserved the quality of *symmetria* most studiously (*diligentissime custodiit*) by reinterpreting traditional geometrical proportions used for the human figure (*Nat.* 34.65). Pliny's account credits Lysippus for also paying attention to even the tiniest parts of his works. In this, he outranks not only Myron, but also Pythagoras from Rhegium who was famously proficient at the representation of small particulars.[24] While the accuracy of Myron and Pythagoras is relative to that of other artists—the former is presented as more careful (*diligentior*) than Polyclitus, while the latter is seen as able to depict details more carefully (*diligentius*) than Myron—Lysippus seems to have reached the peak in this quality (*diligentissime*).

The section about Lysippus is not alone in combining two key critical terms used to introduce the art of Myron. Pliny again associates the two qualities characteristic of Myron, *numerosus* (rich in rhythms) and *diligens* (assiduous), in comments about Antidotus, a painter believed to be a student of Euphranor and a teacher of Nicias who flourished in the mid-fourth century BCE (*Nat.* 35.130).[25] Pliny remembers Antidotus as *diligentior quam numerosior*, a comment that has been variously interpreted as referring either to his productivity (more laborious than prolific) or to his approach to artistic creation (more meticulous than interested in the rhythms of composition).[26] The remark that follows seems to support the latter reading. Pliny explains that he was also "severe in his use of colours" (*in coloribus severus*). In other words, Antidotus followed his teacher Euphranor in seeking to bestow an aura of stateliness on his figures by avoiding subtle gradations of colours. Indeed, the short presentation of Antidotus closely mirrors those of Euphranor and Nicias, the masters with whom Antidotus shared a line of artistic filiation. Like Euphranor, Antidotus deserves praise for his industriousness (*Nat.* 35.128, *laboriosus*). Euphranor is allegedly the first "to have achieved good proportions" (*primus videtur* [...] *usurpasse symmetrian*), although the bodies he painted still appeared too slight with heads and joints that were too sturdy. His student Antidotus also failed to achieve perfection in the use of measures (*numeri*). Antidotus aimed to represent the *dignitas* of his subjects just as Euphranor

had, choosing lofty simplicity and restraint in the use of colours. Antidotus' pupil, Nicias, shared his predecessors' *diligentia*. But unlike
them, Nicias concentrated on the nuanced representation of light and
shadow (*Nat.* 35.130–131).

The concept of *diligentia* (assiduousness) corresponds to the Greek
idea of ἀκρίβεια and holds an important place in Pliny's discourse
on the figural arts.[27] Throughout the *Natural History*, the adjective
diligens and the adverb *diligenter* often appear in comparative or superlative forms, organising sculptors and painters into a hierarchy of
devotion to their work. The question of care in pursuing one's creative
goals is of crucial importance in the *Natural History*, far beyond the
articulation of discourse about the figural arts.

Comparison between the art of Protogenes and Apelles, two
late-Classical painters who took profoundly different approaches to
art, is constructed based on their idea of finiteness (*Nat.* 35.80). The
former is the author of "immensely laborious and infinitely meticulous" works, while the latter is believed keenly aware "of the frequently
evil effect of excessive diligence" (*nocere saepe nimiam diligentiam*).
Unlike Apelles, Protogenes is depicted as impossibly dissatisfied with
himself (*Nat.* 35.102–103) to the point where he abandoned the picture
that would become his most celebrated masterpiece, the hero *Ialysus*,
which he completed later only by virtue of a fortuitous accident.

The drawbacks of diligence become even more explicit in the case
of Apollodorus and Callimachus, two artists whose most memorable 'achievement' appears to be a fastidious precision that frustrated
rather than assisted their creative projects.[28] A man of unrivalled devotion to his art (*diligentissimum*), Apollodorus was a famously uncompromising critic of his own work, wholly unable to satisfy his
consuming passion to the point of destroying his own finished (*perfecta*) statues (*Nat.* 34.81).[29] Given this behaviour, his nickname "the
Madman" is hardly surprising (*insanum cognominatum*). A few paragraphs later, Callimachus is introduced in very similar terms (*Nat.*
34.92). His popularity depended on an unusual epithet bestowed on
him: *catatexitechnus* or "the Niggler"[30]. A notorious detractor of his
own creations, Callimachus was likewise incapable of satiating his
longing for exactitude (*nec finem habentis diligentiae*). His statues were
carefully executed, yet assiduity spoiled their charm entirely (*gratiam
omnem diligentia abstulerit*). In contrast, Apelles' χάρις (the Greek
equivalent for the Latin *gratia*, *Nat.* 35.79) coincided with that master's
simplicity (*Nat.* 35.80) and his ability to "take his hand away from a
picture" at the right moment.

Scattered throughout Books 34 and 35, these paragraphs construct
a conceptual opposition between poles of grace and diligence. Within

the framework of the *Natural History*, artistic creation is constructed as an explicit parallel to Pliny's encyclopaedic programme. The parallel begins with the *Preface*, where Pliny famously expresses the view that any work of art is as endlessly incomplete as his own encyclopaedia (*Praef.* 26). The success of creation rests on a delicate balance between selection and completeness or, in art-historical terms, between *gratia* and *diligentia*.

The art of competition

Pliny recognises an idea of progress within the emergence of increasingly more realistic proportions and the careful representation of details. While the *Natural History*'s presentation of the visual arts upholds an overarching evolutionary pattern, Pliny's discussion of tangible technical skills (*ars*) and the intellectual aspects of creation (*ingenium*) is hardly forthright. In the sections on sculpture and painting, Pliny relies on an evolutionary theory, within which individual artists feature as examples of certain stages of development. But this organising principle is limited to an account of Greek art, which Pliny presents as a history of technical achievements gradually leading to perfection. When discussing artworks produced in Italy and in Rome, instead, he highlights the remote origins of both sculpture and painting in that geographical region (*Nat.* 34.33–34 and 35.17). Rather than concentrating on technical facts, the paragraphs about Italy first establish the venerability of Roman traditions and then concentrate on social aspects such as the reception, use, status, and reputation of certain artefacts, materials, and typologies.[31] When it comes to the role of art in his own cultural environment, Pliny resorts more robustly to the ethical perspective that informs the entire encyclopaedia.

The idea of progress (and the tension that progress generates) allows Pliny to organise his subject matter according to a logical rationale. Throughout the treatise, competition emerges as an important narrative strategy used to visualise, dramatise, and explain internal hierarchies as well as historical sequences.[32] In the final books and especially when discussing painting and sculpture, the narrative unfolds through passages about the key figures among the great masters, often in competition with each other and capable of extraordinary innovations, followed by the lists of their less talented contemporaries, who strived to achieve similar results.

Within this framework, the concept of imitation occupies a central position. Pliny's interest in exploring the scope and limits of imitation emerges in his presentation of Lysippus, an artist who famously based his research into the proportions of the human body on the notion that "it was Nature herself, not an artist, whom one ought to imitate" (*Nat.* 34.61).[33] His sons and pupils were apparently unable to share the same approach, as even the most talented among them, Euthycrates (*Nat.* 34.66), could imitate (*imitatus*) his father's perseverance (*constantia*) but fell short of reaching his elegance (*elegantia*). The notion that the development of art culminated in the age of Alexander the Great, and that later artists would be unable to reach comparable heights, is made even clearer in the section about Apelles, "who surpassed all the painters that preceded and all who were to come after him" (*Nat.* 35.79).[34] In the evolution of the figural arts as described by Pliny, the characters of Apelles and Lysippus are constructed as both points of rupture and unattainable models. In particular, Apelles is credited with technical advancements useful to all other artists, as well as some "which nobody was able to imitate", such as the practice of applying on his finished works (*absoluta opera*) a dark layer of varnish (*Nat.* 35.97: *imitari nemo potuit*).[35]

Pliny returns to the impossible task of imitating extraordinary technical feats with the work of a painter, Pausias, who was a contemporary of Apelles and a student of the same *praeceptor*, Pamphilus (*Nat.* 35.123). Like Apelles, Pausias invented a technique that many others strove to replicate, consisting of a skilful management of light and shading to convey the impression of depth (*Nat.* 35.126). The section about Pausias closes with a lengthy description of this method; his invention is said to have been imitated by many (*imitati sunt multi*) but could not be actually reproduced by anyone (*aequavit nemo*). Within the *Natural History*, Pliny consistently returns to the idea expressed in words such as *aequalitas*, 'sameness, equivalence', *aequalis*, 'equal' (but also 'coeval'), and *aequare*, 'to put (two or more people or their accomplishments) on a level' in order to express artistic hierarchies.[36] Within the field of art, this concept functions as a narrative tool to arrange persons and objects in a sequence. It also establishes ranks among a group of artists from the same period.[37] This is the case with Myron and Polyclitus, who are believed to be contemporaries and pupils of Hagelades (*Nat.* 34.10: *aequales atque condiscipuli*). In Pliny's account, their rivalry (*aemulatio*) extended to the choice of material; Myron used a bronze alloy typical of Aegina, while Polyclitus used a Delian alloy.[38] The entire section devoted to these masters is shaped as a comparison, which extends to a third artist of the same period and level (*Nat.* 34.49, 68), Pythagoras from Rhegium, who was considered superior to Myron in the reproduction of details (*Nat.* 34.59).

In the *Natural History*, rivalry is generally articulated as emblematic of the relationship between artists of the same period. But there is one instance (*Nat.* 34.47) where Pliny makes an exception to introduce an artist from his own time, Zenodorus, who was capable of copying (*aemulatus est*) the work of a Classical master so skilfully that "there was scarcely any difference in artistry" (*Nat.* 34.47).[39] Significantly, the passage is one of only two points in the *Natural History* where Pliny acknowledges the possibility that some of his contemporaries may have equalled the famed masters of the Greek past. In Book 35, the painter entrusted by Vespasian with restorations to the Temple of Honour and Virtue, Attius Priscus, is said to be *antiquis similior* in comparison to other craftsmen of his time (*Nat.* 35.120).[40] It is hardly surprising that Pliny would extol an artist whose *auctoritas* rests on his work in the service of Vespasian. But praise of Zenodorus, the author of Nero's Colossus, is much less straightforward.[41] Here, Pliny sets the artist and his work in opposition (*Nat.* 34.46): the former is by no means inferior to the old masters in his knowledge of modelling and chasing (*scientia fingendi caelandique nulli veterum postponeretur*), while the latter ostensibly demonstrates that the art of casting bronze is now lost (*ea statua indicavit interisse fundendi aeris scientiam*).[42] Insistence on both the merits of the artist and the shortcomings of the Colossus is symptomatic of the contradictions in Pliny's view of history, which sways between the denunciation of moral decadence and praise for Flavian Rome. The section about Zenodorus combines criticism of the most conspicuous symbol of Nero's arrogance (his colossal portrait) with homage to one of the landmarks of the Flavian city (the Colossus of the Sun), which were one and the same. Pliny remarks in *Nat.* 34.45 that "now, dedicated to the Sun", the Colossus "is an object of awe". As part of a broader account on the idea of artistic progress and regress, Zenodorus' remarkable *ars* and the *obliteratio* of the art of casting bronze statues coexist within the same narrative.

Notes

1 See Becatti 1951, 184–185. Scholars have traditionally connected the 'evolutionary' passages in Pliny's account of the figural arts with the work of Xenocrates: Schweitzer 1932, 48; Ferri 1940 and 1942a, 70, 76–78; E. Sellers in Pliny-Jex-Blake, Sellers 1968, xvi–xvii; A. Corso in Pliny-Conte 1982–1988, V, 179. Sprigath 2000 highlights instead the commonplace nature of the evolutionary *topos* in the discourse about the visual art, thus re-framing the role of Xenocrates and the degree of his innovative approach to the topic. For the development of bronze sculpture according to Pliny's *Natural History*, see Isager 1991, 97–103. For the concept of πρῶτος εὑρετής in Greek thought, see Kleingünther 1933.
2 For judgement of Polyclitus' art in the ancient literary sources, see Papini 2018; Adornato 2019b. On *Nat.* 34.56, see Pliny-Ferri 2000, 100–102 note 56; Ferri 1940; 1942a, 76–78; 1965; Harari 2000b, 33–34.

3 A useful introduction to the language of the *Natural History* is Pinkster 2005. For an excellent discussion of Pliny's approach to technical terminology, see Fögen 2010b.

4 H. Rackham (in Pliny-Rackham 1961, 171) renders *multiplicasse veritatem* as "to have enlarged the scope of realism", *numerosior* as "being more prolific", and *in symmetria diligentior* as "being more careful in his proportions". For other translators' approach to this passage, see Pliny-Jex-Blake, Sellers 1968, 47: "He was apparently the first to multiply truth; he was more productive than Polykleitos, and a more diligent observer of symmetry"; Pliny-König, Bayer 1989, 59: "Dieser Myron scheint der erste gewesen zu sein, der sich um mehr Naturtreue bemühte, mehr Harmonie in die Kunst brachte als Polykleitos und sorgfältiger im Ebenmaß war"; Pliny-Le Bonniec, Gallet de Santerre 1983, 128: "semble avoir été le premier à multiplier la vérité des types; ses attitudes sont plus harmonieuses, et ses proportions plus exactes que celles de Polyclète"; Pliny-Ferri 2000, 103, 105: "sembra che Myron sia stato il primo a moltiplicare—segmentandola e scomponendola—la verità, più vario di ritmi rispetto a Polykleitos e più scrupoloso in fatto di simmetria". Ferri's translation is accepted in Pliny-Conte 1982–1988, V, 179. On the problems that the expressions *multiplicasse veritatem* and *numerosior* pose to Pliny's translators, see Pollitt 1974, 135, 411.

5 On ἀλήθεια/*veritas*, see Pollitt 1974, 125–138 (esp. 134–137 for Pliny's passage about Myron). For more recent work, see Adornato 2007 and 2015.

6 For the rhetorical *topos* likening the style of oratory to painting and statuary, see e.g., Demetrius, *On Style* 1.14; Cicero, *On the Orator* 3.26, *Brutus* 70; Dionysius of Halicarnassus, *Isaeus* 4, *Isocrates* 3, *Dinarchus* 7; Quintilian, *Institutes of Oratory* 2.13.10 and 12.10.3–9. For the role of the visual arts in the rhetorical work by Cicero and Quintilian, see Leen 1991 and Austin 1944, respectively.

7 On the identity of critical categories in the Greek and Latin sources about oratory and the visual arts, see Ferri 1942b; Koch 2000–2003. For ancient discourse on the figural arts, see Pollitt 1974; Preisshofen 1979, 273–276; Settis 1992; Bäbler 2002; Tanner 2006; De Angelis 2015; Steiner 2015.

8 Quintilian, *Institutes of Oratory* 7.1.29 and 8.4.27.

9 See also Dionysius of Halicarnassus, *Thucidides* 24, 29, 35, 46.

10 This reading was first advocated in Ferri 1940, 143–154; 1942a, 78–79; Pliny-Ferri 2000, 103–104.

11 For this definition, see Pollitt 1974, 135.

12 Cicero, *Orator* 67 and 170; Quintilian, *Institutes of Oratory* 9.4.45. On ῥυθμός/*numerus*, see Wolf 1955; Giannecchini 1981–1982, esp. 99–100; Formarier 2013. See also Pollitt 1974, 218–228, 409–415; Pucci 2004–2005.

13 See Formarier 2013, 139.

14 Quintilian addresses the difference between *numeri* and *metra* in *Institutes of Oratory* 9.4.45–46.

15 Also *Orator* 166 and 174, see Formarier 2013, 141–142.

16 The form *numerosa tabula* in *Nat.* 35.138 has been consistently interpreted as referring to a crowded picture, see Pliny-Jex-Blake, Sellers 1968, 163; Pliny-Rackham 1961, 363; Pliny-Croisille 1985, 95; Pliny-Conte 1982–1988, V, 451; Pliny-Ferri 2000, 243; Pliny-König, Winkler 2007, 107.

17 Pollitt 1974, 14–22, 256–258. On the intersections between *symmetria* and the Stoic idea of beauty, see also Celkyte 2017; Horn 1989. An evolution

based on the improvement of proportions runs through Pliny's treatment of painting as well (*Nat.* 35.67, 107, 128).

18 For Vitruvius' theory of *symmetria*, see Wilson Jones 2015, 47–48; Gros 1989.

19 E.g., Ashmolean Museum (relief from Samos) and Piraeus Museum, inv. no. 5352 (relief from Salamis), see Dekoulakou-Sideris 1990; Wilson Jones 2000 and 2001; Porter 2010, 440–444.

20 E.g., *Nat. Praef.* 13, 7.76, 21.48, 21.52, 33.49. On the role of Greek vocabulary in the *Natural History*, see Manzoni 1986, 182–199; Fögen 2016. On Pliny's use of Greek words in the field of the figural arts, see Ferri 1942a, 73.

21 In the final five books, see e.g., *Nat.* 34.16, 18, 35; 35.29, 79, 98, 125; 37.11.

22 Cf. Quintilian, *Institutes of Oratory* 12.10.7 for Myron's position in the development of Greek sculpture. For the passages by Cicero and Quintilian, see Adornato 2019a, 566–568; 2019c, 298–300. In *Institutes of Oratory* 11.1.2, Quintilian defines the forms of expression that display a conspicuous rhythmical structure as 'elaborate' (*verba* [...] *figuris etiam numerisque elaborata*).

23 For the replica series of the *Discobolus*, see Anguissola 2005 and 2007a.

24 Diogenes Laertius, *Lives of Eminent Philosophers* 8.47 comments that Pythagoras "is thought to have been the first to aim at rhythm and symmetry" (πρῶτον δοκοῦντα ῥυθμοῦ καὶ συμμετρίας ἐστοχάσθαι).

25 See Koch 2000, 112–113.

26 For the first reading, see Pliny-Jex-Blake, Sellers 1968, 155 ("a laborious rather than a prolific artist"); Pliny-Rackham 1961, 357 ("more careful in his work than prolific"); Pliny-König, Winkler 2007, 101 ("Seine Arbeiten waren mehr sorgfältig als zahlreich"). The passage is translated according to the second line of thought in Pliny-Ferri 2000, 237 ("più diligente che vario nei ritmi", accepted by R. Mugellesi in Pliny-Conte 1982–1988, V, 437); H. Mielsch in *DNO*, no. 2804 ("Er selbst richtete seine Aufmerksamkeit stärker auf die Sorgfalt [der Gestaltung im Detail] als auf die Symmetrie der Komposition"); Pliny-Croisille 1985, 91 ("Antidotus lui-même fut plus soucieux de la précision qu'harmonieux"). On Antidotus, see A. Corso in Pliny-Conte 1982–1988, V, 437 note 2, 870.

27 See, e.g., *Nat.* 34.58, 59, 65, 92; 35.65, 130, 137. On the meaning of *diligentia*, see Perry 2000, esp. 452–454; Ferri 1942a, 88–89 and 1960; Sassi 1994; Pollitt 1974, 351–357. Its Greek counterpart ἀκρίβεια is frequently used in ekphrastic passages (see, e.g., Lucian, *Zeuxis* 3, 5, 7; *The Hall* 9; *Images* 7), see Schwyzer 1923; Kurz 1970; Pollitt 1974, 117–125, 351–357. In her seminal article, Ellen E. Perry warned that in the Roman criticism of art, the notion of *diligentia* cannot always be explained as the equivalent of ἀκρίβεια. Sometimes, it is closer to πόνος, 'toil' (Perry 2000). In *Nat.* 35.137 Pliny is adamant that the quality of *diligentia* belongs to the sphere of 'professional criticism', a feature that "only artists can appreciate".

28 *DNO*, nos. 1578–1588 (last quarter of the fifth century BCE) and nos. 1179–1184 (second half of the fifth century BCE).

29 One cannot fail to notice the contrast that Pliny creates around the concept of 'perfection'. While *perfecta* from an objective standpoint (insofar as there is one, as Chapter 5 will argue), Apollodorus' statues appeared incomplete to their maker.

30 On the meaning of *catatexitechnus*, see Ferri 1942a, 88–89; Pliny-Ferri
    2000, 139; Perry 2000, 454; Pliny-Le Bonniec, Gallet de Santerre, 283 note
    1. Callimachus and his nickname are also mentioned by Vitruvius (*On Ar-
    chitecture* 4.1.10) and Pausanias (*Description of Greece* 1.26.7). Vitruvius'
    account, however, presents this artist in a favourable light, as someone
    who had earned that singular nickname *propter elegantiam et subtilitatem
    artis marmoreae*. According to Pausanias, Callimachus himself had cho-
    sen to be known as κατατηξίτεχνος (which, in this case, should be trans-
    lated as 'the Perfectionist'), having been "the first to drill the stones"
    (λίθους πρῶτος ἐτρύπησε), clearly a uniquely exacting technique.
31 For the role of 'Roman art' in the *Natural History*, see De Angelis 2008,
    esp. 81–82, 87.
32 On Pliny's references to warfare in nature, see Ash 2011, 15–18. On Pliny's
    anecdotes about artistic competition, see Darab 2014a, 214–216.
33 The verb *imitor* occurs 12 times and the noun *imitatio* once in Books 34–
    36. Only twice do they refer to the imitation of a specific artwork, which
    proves to be impossible (*Nat.* 35.63 and 36.85).
34 The narratives that follow the sections about Lysippus and Apelles are
    arranged according to neither the chronological order of artists nor stylis-
    tic development. After the elaboration on the two masters that mark art's
    consummation, the presentation progresses at a rather desultory pace
    based on individual characteristics and achievements, see Isager 1991,
    101–102, 129–130.
35 See Daneu Lattanzi 1982, 105–106. For the technique of *atramentum*, see
    Gage 1981.
36 In two instances, *aequalis* points to an individual artist's consistent qual-
    ity: *Nat.* 35.128 and 36.19.
37 In the case of Praxiteles and Scopas, competition extends to their work,
    see *Nat.* 36.20 and 26.
38 On the meaning of *aemulatio*, *aemulari* and *aemulus* in the final books of
    the *Natural History*, see e.g., *Nat.* 34.49, 35.64, 35.87, 35.95, 35.124, 36.30,
    36.75. In two instances, these words indicate works that no other artists
    could imitate (*Nat.* 34.54 and 71).
39 Pliny mentions Zenodorus' feat of copying (*aemulatus est*) two cups made
    by Calamis, a bronze sculptor and engraver from the fifth century BCE.
    Regardless of the likelihood that Calamis produced the original vessels,
    what is significant here is that Pliny's presentation of Zenodorus revolves
    around his ability to imitate the work of ancient Greek artists, particu-
    larly someone such as Calamis, whose masterpieces famously resisted any
    attempts at emulation (*Nat.* 34.71).
40 In referring to artworks, Pliny employs similar terms for the statue of
    Venus dedicated in the Templum Pacis, *antiquorum dignam fama*.
41 For Pliny's visit to the workshop of Zenodorus see Cook 2020; Anguissola
    2006 (esp. 561–565 with regard to Pliny's choice of words to highlight the
    emotional dimension of the event); Carey 2003, 156–158; Zimmer 1985,
    43–44.
42 See also *Nat.* 34.47: "The greater was the eminence (*praestantia*) of Zeno-
    dorus, the more we realise how the art of working bronze has deteriorated
    (*aeris obliteratio*)".

Part II
The process of art

4 Discovering art

Laquearia, quae nunc et in privatis domibus auro teguntur, post Carthaginem eversam primo in Capitolio inaurata sunt censura L. Mummi. Inde transiere in camaras quoque et parietes, qui iam et ipsi tamquam vasa inaurantur, cum varie sua aetas de Catulo existimaverit, quod tegulas aereas Capitoli inaurasset.

(*Natural History* 33.57)

Pliny's reservations regarding the practice of gilding are by no means limited to the use of precious veneers on bronze and marble statues, as discussed in Chapter 2. The taste for silver vessels plated or inlaid with gold (*Nat.* 33.49), as well as for the *inauratio* of the walls of private houses (*Nat.* 35.2–4), becomes the object of scathing criticism at various points in the *Natural History*. In the opening of Book 35, Pliny castigates indifference towards earnest plasterwork in favour of covering the walls with marble, which are, in turn, embellished with gold leaf (*Nat.* 35.2–4). In a double layer of fabrication, modest plaster is hidden beneath slabs of lavish marble, concealed in turn by gold. A preoccupation with materials' intrinsic value usurps concerns regarding artisanal expertise and finesse.

The section from Book 33 which constitutes this chapter's starting point adds two significant elements to the argument. First, Pliny treats the 'misuse of gold' as a broader cultural phenomenon, which likewise applies to other materials and media. Second, he describes the progress of this technique from the public (sacred) to the private sphere: from the roofs of temples to the ceilings (*laquearia*), vaults (*in camaras*), and walls (*parietes*) of houses. The shift in fashion is linked with an opulent 'aesthetic of ambiguity', which, according to Pliny's explanation in *Nat.* 35.2–3, began with the introduction of marble *crustae* on walls. Removing stones from the vast expanses of the mountains to use

DOI: 10.4324/9780429329159-4

them in interior decoration, thereby subverting the relationship between natural landscapes and artificial indoor spaces, is the first stage
in the corruption of taste. This practice evolves in deceptive strategies
like using golden veneers, and finally the imitation of painted images
by means of stone inlays (*lapide pingere*).[1]

Presumably, Pliny's objection is not aimed at the technique of gilding in itself, but at certain *contexts* and *associations* of its employment.[2]
Pliny's interest in innovation aligns with the work's purpose, to com-
pile a comprehensive body of knowledge encompassing both Rome's
venerable traditions and the advancements enabled by the almost
boundless expansion of the empire (*Praef.* 15).[3] In this light, investigating the ways in which innovation in the field of the figural arts is
presented and discussed may shed light on Pliny's intellectual project
and his organising principles. Thus, we may ask: what is the relationship between progress and history, as well as between progress and
the place towards which, on Pliny's account, everything converges,
the city of Rome? Moreover, how does the narrative about artists
and artworks intersect with Pliny's concerns regarding technological
innovation? Finally, what is the role of Nature—the encyclopaedia's
ultimate object—in enabling and assisting human progress?

Invention and authority

In *Nat.* 33.57, Pliny locates the introduction of gilding in the Republican period, following the fall of Corinth and Carthage in 146 BCE,
when Rome became hegemonic in the Mediterranean.[4] Changes in
domestic taste led to the use of gilding *in privatis domibus*, which is
said to have happened immediately before and during the reign of
Nero, in a climate characterised by an appetite for increasingly artificial, deceptive solutions (*Nat.* 35.2–3). Throughout the *Natural History*,
Pliny is characteristically precise in detailing when a certain technique, object, or resource became known or entered into use in Rome.[5]
He also connects—in a nexus of causes and effects—discoveries and
novel trends in fashion with Rome's political landscape, its protago-
nists, and their ethical approaches.

This strategy is consistent with Pliny's wish to present his information as reliable, as well as with his work's overall project, according
to which innovation and the trajectory of Rome's expansion are inextricably intertwined.[6] While Pliny is steadfast in his belief in progress
(*Nat.* 2.62), he nevertheless dwells on the apparent contradiction between the peaceful and industrious atmosphere fostered by the Flavian
dynasty and his contemporaries' indifference towards the pursuit of

research (*Nat.* 2.117–118).[7] Pliny explains this perceived asymmetry through a moral lens, as the consequence of a relaxation of customs (*avaritia*), which causes people to value profit (*lucrum*) over knowledge (*scientia*).[8] The encyclopaedist blames his contemporaries as appreciative exclusively of the kind of innovation aimed at satisfying idle vanity and extravagant tastes.

Pliny's own resistance to this decline coincides with his encyclopaedic enterprise, which at once revives ancestral traditions and legitimises more recent innovations in an implicit bid to make the Roman public aware of the exceptional possibilities afforded to them under Flavian rule. The bonding agent—and the source of authority—for the multitude of both old and new discoveries collected in the encyclopaedia is their connection with Rome. Rome is presented in continuity with the Hellenistic kingdoms: the beneficiary of their achievements in matters of science and experience.[9] Cartographic projects such as 'Agrippa's map', displayed in the *Porticus Vipsania* and a fundamental reference in Pliny's geography, were the product of the progressive amplification of the world known to the Romans.[10] Pliny introduces each animal by detailing when that species was first seen in Rome (e.g., *Nat.* 8.69), typically as part of the booty paraded during a triumph or among the beasts displayed in the circus.[11] The same fate befalls plants and herbs, which were sent to the emperors from remote corners of the world, exhibited in triumphal procession, and dedicated in the most prominent spots in Rome.[12] Collective experience of new substances and creatures in institutional frameworks functions as a 'confirmative strategy', replacing abstract knowledge with first-hand, verified observation. This experience is central to the incorporation of recent discoveries into the larger body of Roman knowledge, as well as to their commodification.

The story regarding the balsam shrub, which was unique to the region of Judaea, is exemplary in this respect (*Nat.* 12.111–113).[13] This species was first displayed (*ostendere*) in the capital by Vespasian and Titus following the conquest of Jerusalem. Just like the people who inhabited that land, balsam too is "now a subject of Rome".[14] This substance's servile status becomes a precondition of its knowability: only after being brought to Rome does balsam become available for inspection, evincing radically different characteristics (*in totum alia natura*) than what had been assumed before. In its turn, knowledge provides the premises for the exploitation of balsam in the name of collective utility, cultivated under the supervision of the public treasury (*fiscus*).[15] Through its biography, balsam had become synonymous with its land of origin and, as such, was intrinsically linked with the

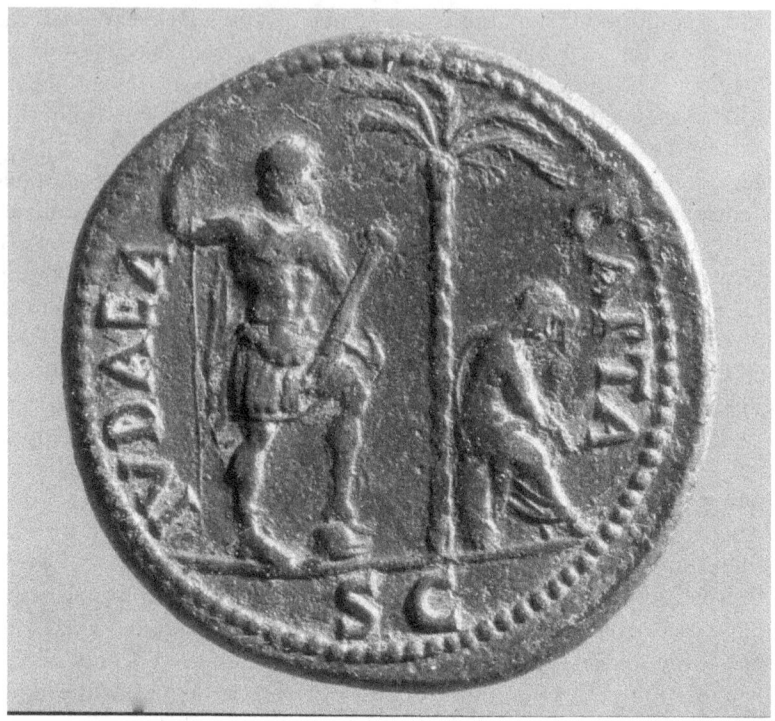

Figure 4.1 Coin (sestertius) of Titus, 80 CE. Bronze. Diametre 35.5 mm, weight 25.45 gr. Reverse: mourning woman beside a palm tree beside Titus, with the inscription *IVDAEA CAPTA*, "Judaea conquered". Jerusalem, The Israel Museum, acc. no. 92.005.14274.
Credit: Bridgeman Images.

history of Roman power (Figure 4.1). In Pliny's narrative the *individual* biography of objects that initially allowed them to be singled out and transformed into metaphors of power coalesced into the cultural life of *all items* conveyed to Rome during its expansion.[16]

The role of emperors in the progress of Roman knowledge is to collect information and resources from the fringes of their dominion and promote research about their properties and uses.[17] The emperor's prerogatives were extensive, from the possibility of controlling the circulation of new knowledge, all the way to the ultimate choice to curb innovation.[18] Pliny's account of glass highlights this point (*Nat.* 36.189–195). He introduces this section in a familiar way: mentioning the emergence of a new technique, glass mosaic for the walls and vaults of buildings, which requires a broader explanation about the "nature of glass". Relying upon his readers' knowledge, Pliny does not describe the physical properties of glass, focusing instead on the provenance of the sand used to produce this material and its evolving techniques.[19] A curious tale about the discovery of a method for working glass "so as to render it flexible" concludes the discussion (*Nat.* 36.195). On that account, under Tiberius the entire workshop that invented the 'unbreakable glass' was destroyed, "for fear that the value of metals such as copper, silver and gold would otherwise be lowered". A few years earlier, the same tale had been included in Petronius' *Cena Trimalchionis* (*Satyricon* 51) and it would later feature in Cassius Dio's historical volumes (*Roman History* 57.21).[20] Cassius Dio makes no mention of an extraordinary invention (the event rather resembles a trick by a craftsman anxious to impress the emperor) and presents the story from an exclusively moral perspective as an instance of Tiberius' resentful nature.[21] The accounts by Petronius and Pliny, instead, share important similarities. Despite differences in tone, both authors describe an alleged technological improvement, explaining Tiberius' hostility as an attempt to protect the selling price of metals. In order to avoid devaluing other materials, in Petronius' dramatised folktale the emperor had the *faber* beheaded, while Plinius' sober version mentions the destruction of the man's *officina*, the location where the invention took place and where traces of its process may remain for others to exploit. Petronius implicitly dismisses the veracity of this anecdote by attributing it to Trimalchio: the consummate hyperbolic and unreliable narrator. Pliny, who is committed to giving his readers a faithful account, uses a carefully detached tone. He mentions having learned about this story from hearsay, avoids blaming Tiberius explicitly as responsible for the workshop's destruction, and remarks that the story has enjoyed a popularity far exceeding its credibility. Pliny's discussion of glass ends with the report of another—equally upsetting for the market—invention: a technique enabling the convincing imitation of rock crystal.[22] Like many other 'useless' discoveries, the *petrotoi* vessels ('stoneware') had been introduced under Nero; at this time, according to Pliny's moralistic perspective, the ethical connection between innovation and utility had been substituted for one of novelty and indulgence. Far from being a *trigger* of social and economic change, in Pliny's view, technological progress constituted a *consequence* of political circumstances and the state of society. Thus, technological advancements are not a driving force for history but a product of political authority and a mirror for collective morals.

The place for innovation

Pliny connects the technological innovation of gilded ceilings with a time and place: the censorship of Lucius Mummius after the fall of Carthage (and Corinth) and the Capitoline temple. In the books dedicated to the materials of art, Lucius Mummius is depicted as a pivotal figure in the process of assimilating Greek art in Rome that took place during the second century BCE.[23] Pliny dramatises this process by drawing upon a familiar body of caricatural anecdotes regarding Mummius' alleged ignorance about art in a way to convey the intellectual and emotional dimension of the encounter between the Roman elite and the art of the Greeks.[24] A famous passage epitomises the magnitude of the challenge, as well as the fluctuating relationship between price and value in the *Natural History* (*Nat.* 35.24). When the booty captured from Corinth was put on sale, the king of Pergamon—Attalus II—purportedly offered to pay the hyperbolic sum of 600,000 *denarii* for a picture made by the fourth-century BCE master Aristides of Thebes. Surprised by Attalus' bid and suspecting that "there must be some merit in the picture of which he was himself unaware", Mummius had the picture recalled from the auction.[25]

In Pliny's account, this event marks a turn in the course of history, since it bestows for the first time an aura of authority onto paintings by foreign masters. Mummius had succeeded in gaining recognition for these pieces by dedicating the picture by Aristides in the Temple of Ceres in Rome, which was the first instance, Pliny believed, "of a foreign picture becoming state-property at Rome".[26] This decisive event which, around a century later, attached outstanding meaning (*praecipua auctoritas*) to the art of painting in the collective perception of the Romans is said to have been equally entangled in pecuniary questions (*Nat.* 35.26). Julius Caesar purchased the pictures of *Ajax* and *Medea* by the contemporary painter Timomachus of Byzantium for no less than 80 Attic talents (roughly 480,000 *denarii*, on Varro's calculations) and placed them before the Temple of Venus Genetrix.[27] The picture of *Medea*, being Timomachus' final work, was left unfinished, adding to the painting's mystique (*Nat.* 35.145). In Pliny's narrative, the temples of Rome are places where new items may be liberated from prior associations and vested with a new 'fully Roman' identity, thereby becoming part of collective memory and practice.[28]

Throughout Pliny's account of the figural arts, 'origin' constitutes an essential organising principle. Each technology or medium is introduced with reference to its most ancient specimen, viz. the earliest instance known to Rome. Pliny draws all of these pivotal examples from the sacred sphere, preferably in Rome.[29] Of course, Roman generals and emperors had dedicated valuable and extraordinary objects in temples and sanctuaries for centuries. Nonetheless, by resorting to this kind of evidence, Pliny seems to depend on narrative concerns in addition to reflecting historical reality. On the one hand, reference to famous sacred contexts may corroborate his information, emphasising Roman dominion over material, intellectual, and artistic resources. On the other hand, the mention of venerable sacred places draws on a repository of shared knowledge and allows Pliny to smoothly introduce names and details that may be less familiar to his readers. So, all kinds of innovative objects and techniques seem to have converged over the centuries towards the Capitoline Temple of Jupiter: from architectural gilding (*Nat.* 33.57) to new arrangements for the floor (*Nat.* 36.185), to the first public collection of gems (*Nat.* 37.11), and the first myrrhine bowls ever seen in Rome (*Nat.* 37.18).

In light of these remarks, we may reconsider the passage cited at the beginning of this chapter. Pliny presents gilding—the most valuable of all veneers—as an exemplar of *luxuria* and a key factor in the loss of both artistic skill and sensitive appreciation of all media (*Nat.* 33.49 and 57, 34.63, 35.2).[30] Pliny's contumely, however, is limited to the *contemporary* uses of gilding for private, hedonic purposes. When applied to public enjoyment in the sacred (and, thus, *traditional*) sphere, the same techniques seem not only to be *acceptable* (as is the case with the ceilings in the Capitoline Temple, as well as the gilded *simulacrum* of Fortuna in the sanctuary of Praeneste, mentioned at *Nat.* 33.61), but also the sign of Rome's ability to assimilate ever-changing technologies. The judgement of artistic materials and techniques articulates along two, intersecting trajectories: those regarding place (public or private); and those regarding time (past or present). Just as sacred spaces warrant appropriation and assimilation owing to their collective function, as well as their embodiment of tradition, so does the encylopaedia—the utilitarian text *par excellence*—serve as the *literary place* where old and new knowledge merges and crystallises. This identification is implicit in the metaphors on which Pliny draws in the *Preface*, especially in explaining the character and ambitions of his work. Quoting an otherwise-unknown Domitius Piso, Pliny compares his own treatise to a *thesaurus* (*Praef.* 17): a Greek word connected with the religious sphere, meaning either a 'hoard of prized objects' dedicated in a sanctuary or the 'storage' in which such items are preserved within a sanctuary.[31] He expands this similitude by turning it into a nod to the dedicatee of his encyclopaedia: the future emperor Titus (*Praef.* 19). Notwithstanding the difficult circumstances in which the work was composed (largely in Pliny's spare time at night), the very choice to dedicate it to Titus is a guarantee of quality in the eye of the public (*haec fiducia operis, haec est indicatura*), since "many objects are deemed extremely precious just because of the fact that they are votive offerings".

The craft of nature

Apparently, the fame bestowed upon the 'first celebrated gem', a sardonyx once belonging to Polycrates of Samos, had little to do with its physical qualities and intrinsic worth (*Nat.* 37.4). The reasons for its fame—and thus its dedication in the Temple of Concordia—lie instead in an extraordinary twist of fate.[32] According to legend, in an act of superstition, the king had decided to surrender a small portion of his riches, in order to atone for his excessive wealth. To do so, he threw the gem into the sea, only for it to be swallowed by a large fish and returned "to its owner in his own kitchen". The main factor in this object's gripping biography is "Fortune's treacherous intervention" (*Fortunae insidiantis manu*).

Fortuitous events seem to hold a special place in Pliny's narrative of discoveries and innovation. In explaining the cultivation of trees, Pliny details a long list of techniques taught to mankind by Nature—*natura docuit* or *natura (de)monstravit* (*Nat.* 17.59, 65, 67, 96, 99, 101).[33] He then proceeds with methods devised by Chance (*casus*), highlighting the difference between the two concepts (*Nat.* 17.101): "so far Nature has herself been our instructor, but grafting was taught us by Chance, another tutor and one who gives us perhaps more frequent lessons".[34] Although both defy human agency, resulting in 'unexpected' discoveries, *natura* possesses a transcendent yet coherent and creative dynamism, while *casus* is either the result of a miscalculation or the unanticipated effect of an action with entirely different purposes. Elsewhere, Pliny is more explicit in discussing the relationship between Nature and Chance: the latter being a function and an expression of the former (*Nat.* 27.8). While Chance (*casus*) is the "great deity (*deus*) who has made most of the discoveries" that improve human life, what in fact is meant by this name is the mother and instructor of all things (*parens rerum omnium et magistra*)—a definition used a few paragraphs earlier to describe Nature (*Nat.* 27.2: *omnium parentem*).

Chance discoveries occupy a central space within Pliny's exploration of the figural arts. The fundamental aspect in the ontology of gems and precious stones is that they are pure and unadulterated products of Nature.[35] Glass, too, is the result of a lucky incident—the unplanned mixing of soda and Phoenician sand under a cauldron (*Nat.* 36.191). Man's contribution is limited to researching new sources for ingredients and more advanced production strategies. The origin story of the coveted 'Corinthian bronze' is strikingly similar (*Nat.* 34.5–6).[36] The Corinthian alloy is said to have resulted from the melting of the city's bronze, silver, and gold treasures "when Corinth was burned at the time of its capture". Apparently, some significant unpredictability remained attached to this technique: one type of Corinthian alloy, *hepatizon* (or 'livery', so-called owing to its colour), "is a blend produced by luck (*fortuna*)" (*Nat.* 34.8).[37] Both glass and Corinthian bronze owe their existence to the power of fire (*Nat.* 36.200–201). Placed at the end of Book 36, the section on fire closes the description of "everything that depends on Man's talent for making Art reproduce Nature" (*ingenio arte naturam faciente*). In the very last paragraph of the book (*Nat.* 36.204), by reminding the reader of the miraculous flame in the home of Tarquinius Priscus that announced the birth of Servius Tullius, Pliny brings his reader back from a kaleidoscope of marvels to the warm intimacy of the hearth and the familiar Roman tradition. In the following book on gems (Book 37), man is little more than a spectator of Nature's creative force.

Occasionally, an artwork is *itself* presented as the product of Chance, in line with widespread visual practices and imagery. A number of objects from Pliny's time attest to an interest in 'miraculous natural images', which exploit the physical qualities of material for representational purposes, as if the outlines of figures and things had been created by Nature herself (Figure 4.2).[38] After briefly sketching the earliest history of marble sculpture, Pliny mentions the preferred medium for all ancient masters: the marble quarried at Paros, where a miracle allegedly took place and a block, split open by the stone-cutters' wedges, revealed the image of Silenus (*Nat.* 36.14).[39] Pliny thereby reminds his readers that "this art is much older than that of painting or of bronze statuary" (*Nat.* 36.15).[40] This intimation of a deep relationship with natural forces—with marble belonging to those 'prohibited' substances that men excavate from the womb of the earth (*Nat.* 36.2)—supports Pliny's argument in favour of a primeval origin of marble sculpture: an art form that relies more on the affordances of Nature than the expertise of craftsmen.

Pliny's narrative of the rivalry between Apelles and his contemporary Protogenes extends to the role of Chance in completing or halting their works. On Apelles' own admission, their achievements were "in all respects […] on a level", except for their relation to finiteness (*Nat.* 35.80). While Apelles instinctively knew "when to take his hand

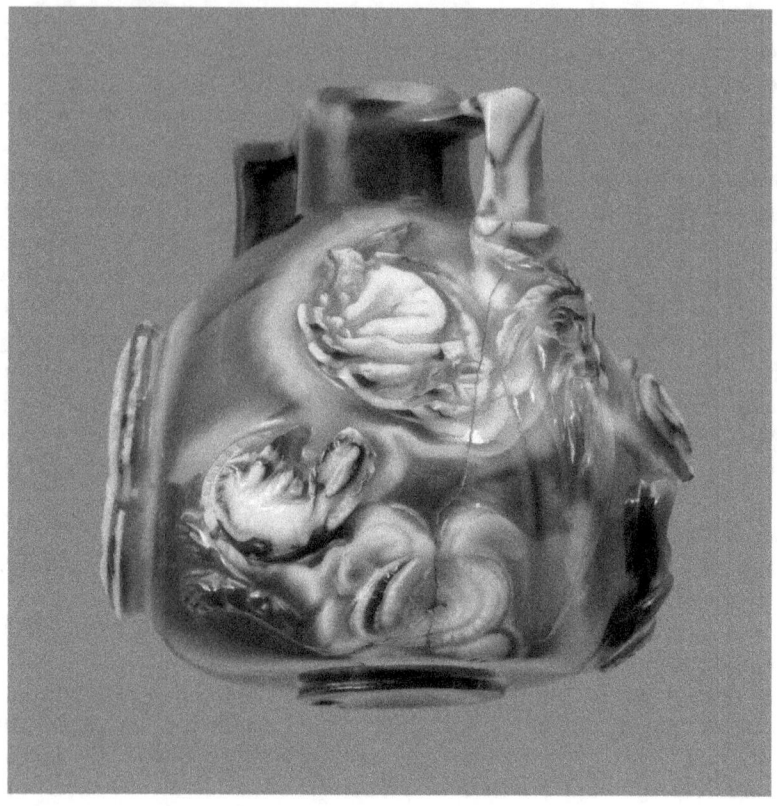

Figure 4.2 Small relief vessel, first-century CE. Agate. H 6 cm, diameter 5.7 cm. Vienna, Kunsthistorisches Museum, Antikensammlung, inv. no. X 22.

Credit: Vienna, Kunsthistorisches Museum, Antikensammlung.

away from a picture", Protogenes was a man of "immensely laborious and infinitely meticulous work". At least for one particular piece
by each master—Apelles' last *Aphrodite* and Protogenes' *Ialysus*—
Chance levelled the playing field in the approach to art. The renown
of Apelles' painting depends on its having been left unfinished at the
death of its master—that is, on its having been left in a state determined by Chance. The famous anecdote about Protogenes' picture of
the hero *Ialysus* (*Nat.* 35.102–103) presents the artist as miserable with
his own meticulousness, which impressed on the painting an air of
artificiality, far from the realism (*veritas*) for which he yearned.[41] The

picture, which had become an unending work-in-progress, was only finished when Protogenes tossed a sponge at the painting in frustration, thereby miraculously attaining the desired effect (*fecitque* [...] *fortuna naturam*). Just as the legend of the Corinthian alloy allows Pliny to explore his contemporaries' greed and make a case for the reprehensible subversion of values, the popular story of Protogenes' *Ialysus* gives occasion for making a moral point. Although his "excessive diligence" made Protogenes the object of his rival's reproach, Pliny seems to construct the painter's laboriousness and forbearance with the infinite possibilities of art as a counterpart to his own industry, knowing well the challenges of 'finishing' his encyclopaedia.[42] The fact that Pliny's readers could see Protogenes' *Ialysus* in Vespasian's *Templum Pacis* would lend 'corporeal presence' to the anecdote, as well as to its value as an *exemplum*.[43] Another similarity links Pliny's stories about the origin of glass and Corinthian bronze to that of Protogenes' masterpiece. In both cases, powerful, ever-mobile natural substances function as the instrument of *fortuna*: fire, on the one hand; a sponge, on the other. With its primordial, instinctive intelligence (*intellectum*, *Nat.* 9.148) for the retention and release of air and liquids, the sponge alleviates and 'corrects' Protogenes' frustrating inability to tune into 'natural' finitude.[44]

Knowledge and creation form part of a gradual process of revelation and learning in which the Stoic Nature, suffused with a vital *pneuma*, displays her "power and majesty" (*Nat.* 7.7).[45] While Nature's agency may defy human comprehension, nothing in the natural world is created without a purpose and everything holds a precise position in the world's scheme (*Nat.* 7.6, 22.1).[46] In the environment around them, men should search for Nature's will instead of reasons that exceed their comprehension (*Nat.* 37.60). As Pliny explains at the beginning of Book 27 on medical herbs, even when a certain innovation appears to constitute the contribution of a single man, the ultimate responsibility for it rests with Nature and her benevolence, for Nature generates and affords inventions to humanity (*Nat.* 27.1–2). Thus, the enigma of creation lies, according to Pliny, in the indefinable ability to be attuned with the generative power of Nature and her *voluntas*.

Notes

1 In *Nat.* 22.4, Pliny reiterates his preference for walls painted with vegetable pigments over the practice of "painting with stone". The discovery and use of mosaics follows a similar progression from the floor of a sanctuary to the ceiling (*Nat.* 36.189).

2 While Pliny allows for the use of certain materials owing to their natural properties (as is the case for marble columns in temple architecture, employed for higher stability, *Nat.* 36.45), he is aware that the introduction of new technologies in the public sphere had often been a cover for private exploitation (*Nat.* 36.5–6, on the marble columns destined to Scaurus' theatre and eventually placed in his house). For criticism of marble columns in private houses, also see *Nat.* 17.6. The *topos* of moderation in the domestic sphere has a robust tradition and the material of columns is used elsewhere as a symbol of restraint or extravagance, see e.g., Suetonius, *Augustus* 72. In *Nat.* 37.18, Pliny details a similar trajectory for myrrhine vases; see also the parallels about bronze in *Nat.* 34.13 and 17.

3 Beagon 1992, 57–68 and Naas 2008 explore Pliny's idea of progress; see also Isager 1991, 33–42 and Citroni Marchetti 1991, 202–204, 230, 237. Discussing the *Natural History* in the context of Roman Imperial geography, Arnaud 2007, 20 comments upon Pliny's challenge in treating innovation "dans le cadre global d'une société où la nouveauté était tout le contraire d'une qualité". Healy 1999 provides an excellent exploration of science and technology in the *Natural History*; see also Badel 2006.

4 Ash 2011, 5–7 emphasises the role of "warfare as a chronological marker" in the *Natural History*. See also Romani Mistretta 2018 for chronological markers in Pliny's account of inventions.

5 Pliny exploits supposedly concomitant events or discoveries to construct a solid chronological framework, see *Nat.* 7.210–215, 34.17, 35.54, 36.15.

6 An entire section of Book 7 on anthropology is dedicated to inventions (*Nat.* 191–215), see Beagon 2005, 416–472; Naas 2002, 321–324.

7 Pliny's explains that "now that every sea has been opened up", a multitude of people is able to travel; yet, they do so in search of profit, not for knowledge. For a similar concept, about seafaring undertaken for the purpose of war or profit, see Seneca, *Natural Questions* (5.18.4–16).

8 Pliny returns to this point in *Nat.* 25.1–2, where he also explores the negative effects of intellectual laziness on the burdensome task of passing knowledge down for posterity, see Citroni Marchetti 2017, 70; Naas 2002, 405–411. See also *Nat.* 15.57 for the idea of 'saturation' in certain spheres of knowledge.

9 This point is made explicit in the story about Mithridates' archive of medical research, which was the result of the king collecting information "from all his subjects, who comprised a great part of the world" (*Nat.* 25.7). After he conquered Mithridates' kingdom, Pompey had the trove of documents translated into Latin, thus claiming a victory that "was as beneficent to life as it was to the State". Control over a large territory is presented as essential to collecting a body of knowledge such as Mithridates'. In turn, Pompey's conquest is instrumental to the security of the State and the well-being of its citizens. Unlike Mithridates, who kept the precious papers among his personal belongings (*in arcanis suis*), Pompey understood the potential of these documents to the common good. Totelin 2012, 133 remarks that, in telling this story, Pliny refers to Mithridates kingdom "as the sum of all the king's subjects (*omnibus subiectis*)", rather than as "a single entity". In consequence, his knowledge also remains an assemblage of individual facts (as Pliny suggests by presenting Mithridates' research with the words *singula exquirens*), instead of contributing to a

larger, coherent totality. For Mithridates' medical collection, see Flemming 2005, 458.

10 On this map, see Dilke 1987, 207–209; Salway 2001, 29; Brodersen 2003, 268–287; Carey 2003, 61–74. Pliny presents the exploration of new territories as a corollary of Roman expansion (*Nat.* 5.9, 11, 51; 6.40, 160, 181). Occasionally, the news of uncharted territories reaches Rome thanks to the travels of diplomatic envoys (*Nat.* 6.84, 140) or merchants (*Nat.* 6.140). For an introduction to Pliny's geography, see Vial-Logeay 2017. For a general overview of geography in early imperial Rome, see Nicolet 1991. See also Cecconi 2007 on the role of military history within the *Natural History*.

11 *Nat.* 8.4, 6, 53, 55, 64, 69, 70, 71; see also *Nat.* 9.14, 10.5. See Carey 2000, 6 and 2003, 84–85. For triumphs and their role in 'dramatising' imperialism and marking the assimilation of the conquered, see Beard 2009, 163–167; Murphy 2004, 157. For Pliny's account of animals, see Bodson 1986; Fögen 2007.

12 Pliny mentions plants being discovered during military campaigns (*Nat.* 12.21), brought to Rome or sent to emperors from remote lands (*Nat.* 12.57; 18.95; 19.39), and thereafter exhibited in prominent places (*Nat.* 12.94 and 16.200). In *Nat.* 12.20, Pliny mentions that the ebony tree was first seen in Rome when Pompey triumphed over Mithridates. In *Nat.* 12.111, he presents Pompey's 'botanical triumph' as the antecedent of Vespasian's own display of the balsam shrub—thus connecting his victorious patron to a figure from the Republican past of Rome discussed in light of the 'universality' of his achievements (*Nat.* 7.93–99; see Beagon 2005, 54–55). Manolaraki 2015, 649–660 considers the idea of a 'botanical contest' between present and past conquerors. On trees in triumphal processions, see Östenberg 2009, 184–188, especially p. 188 regarding Pliny's usage of the verb *ducere*, which is typically employed in connection to moving creatures (on Pliny's tendency "to collapse distinctions between types of objects", see Libonati 2017). On Pliny's botanical books, see Chevallier 1986 and Morton 1986.

13 Manolaraki 2015; Murphy 2004, 162–163; Totelin 2012, 122–125.

14 Östenberg 2009, 279. Pliny's remark that "now" (*nunc*) the balsam is a subject of Rome together with its people is a subtle indication of the author's political allegiances, as he embraces the Flavian narrative and magnifies the scale of the 'conquest', presenting Roman rule in Judaea as a recent, first-time achievement.

15 On the management of the balsam, see Cotton and Eck 1997; Manolaraki 2015, 640–644. The *Natural History* includes several mentions of animals and plants conveyed from remote lands (e.g., *Nat.* 8.222) to Rome, where they thrived and became part of the local environment (*Nat.* 12.112–113).

16 The concept of 'object biographies' provides a tool to examine the ways in which meanings and values are negotiated, accumulated, and modified over time. This notion was first introduced by Igor Kopytoff, who explained (1986, 73) how power can reinforce its own claims by "insisting on its right to singularize an object, or a set or class of objects". See also Fontijn 2013; Hoskins 2006; Godsen and Marshall 1999.

17 In *Nat.* 5.12, Pliny elaborates upon the connection between authority and reliability.

18 Murphy 2004, 197–209. Emperors could accelerate progress (e.g., *Nat.* 7.162) or curb it. Suetonius, *Life of Vespasian* 18 mentions Vespasian's choice not to exploit a new and cheaper method for transporting columns in order to provide work to his poorest subjects, see Casson 1978; Giglioni Bodei 1974, esp. 180–184. In one instance, Pliny includes the story of a new material that allegedly did not come into use because it did not match the taste of the time (*Nat.* 35.57).

19 Freestone 2008 discusses the Roman technology of glass-making in light of Pliny's account.

20 The anecdote is also in Isidore's *Etymologies* (16.16.6), drawing on Petronius' and Pliny's texts. On the versions of this story, see also Santini 1986; Lassen 1995; Murphy 2004, 200–201; Champlin 2008, 411.

21 For the portrait of Tiberius in Cassius Dio's *Roman History*, see Baar 1990.

22 A. Corso in Pliny-Conte 1982–1988, V, 733 note 2; A. Rouveret in Pliny-André, Bloch, Rouveret 1981, 246, note 2. See *Nat.* 36.199 for glass vessels as commercial 'competitors' of silverware. Pliny mentions again the glass imitation of crystal vessels in *Nat.* 37.29, where he seems to correct the information provided in the previous book, stating that the invention did not lower the price of actual crystal.

23 On the Roman acquaintance to Greek artistic tradition, see *Nat.* 33.148–150, 34.12, 34.36, 35.24, and 37.12. Pliny holds the conquest of Asia and Greece as responsible for Rome's moral decline, in line with a long tradition: Polybius, *Histories* 9.10.1–12; Livy, *History of Rome* 25.40.1–2; Plutarch, *Life of Marcellus* 21.1–5. On the Roman encounter with Greek art and the moral dilemmas that it elicited, see Becatti 1951, 9–13; Pollitt 1978; Gruen 1993, 95–101; Miles 2008, 55–73.

24 See Polybius, *Histories* 39.2.1–2; Strabo, *Geography* 8.6.23; Velleius Paterculus, *History of Rome* 1.13.4; Dio Chrysostom, *Discourses* 37.42. In describing Mummius' incompetence on art, Velleius Paterculus mentions an incident that finds a close parallel in Pliny's passage regarding Nero's substitution of Apelles' *Anadyomene*, discussed in Chapter 5. When ordering the removal of the masterpieces looted in Achaia (*maximorum artificum perfectas manibus tabulas ac statuas*), Mummius allegedly ordered the men entrusted with the transportation to substitute any items that would be lost en route to Italy with new ones. The inability to perceive the 'aura' of an original—which coincides with signs of its master's 'hand'—is a *topos* in the construction of inappropriate behaviour towards art. On the portrayal of Mummius by the ancient literary sources, see Gruen 1993, 123–129 and Cadario 2014.

25 García Morcillo 2008, 148–149 argues that auctions, as "ritualised mechanisms of public competition", played an important role towards the shared understanding of art.

26 On the dedications made by Mummius, see Bravi 2012, 44–48 and 2014, 48–54.

27 Cf. *Nat.* 7.126, 35.136. See Bravi 2014, 85–95. On Timomachus' *Medea*, see also Perry 2005, 168–171.

28 Regarding the discursive practices elicited by objects in temples, cf. Platt 2010.

29 E.g., *Nat.* 34.15 (bronze), 35.17–19, 35.22, 35.115–116 (wall painting), 36.13 (marble sculpture) and 189 (mosaic), 37.3–4 (gems). Pliny mentions objects dedicated in sacred contexts because of their technological prowess (*Nat.* 35.161; see also *Nat.* 19.12) or the sheer quantity of a rare material (*Nat.* 36.196, 37.27). The connection between art and the sacred sphere is evident in the case of restoration. With one exception (the removal of Nero's gilding from Lysippus' *Alexander as a Boy*), restoration is always mentioned in the context of sacred possessions (*Nat.* 35.91, 99–100, 120, 154). The stories of artworks that had been repaired are essential to Pliny's endeavour to lend chronological depth to his treatment.

30 In Pliny's discussion, the progression of increasingly complicated applications of a technology culminates with *loss*—that is, in both the ability to use that technology, and to appreciate a craftsman's skill.

31 See Carey 2003, 75–76; Citroni Marchetti 2005a, 112–114.

32 See *Nat.* 33.27 and Citroni Marchetti 2011, 147–171; Platt 2020b. The story of Polycrates' ring originates with Herodotus' *Histories* 3.40–42, about which, see van der Veen 1993. On the display in the Temple of Concordia, see Kellum 1990. Attributing the dedication of the sardonyx to Livia, based on Pliny's text, has been questioned by Hulme 2011.

33 See also *Nat.* 25.16 on the chance discovery of vegetal remedies. Manolaraki 2018, 218–219 discusses the role of *natura* as *artifex* in the *Natural History*. See also Beagon 1992, 63–65.

34 See also *Nat.* 17.123. Under Roman law, *casus* is an accident for which it is impossible to blame a third party, see Jansen 2016. On the symbolism associated with grafting in Roman thought, see Lowe 2010.

35 *Nat.* 37.193 mentions that new precious stones "come into existence quite unexpectedly".

36 Petronius, *Satyricon* 50.5–6 exploits this story to humourous ends, with Trimalchio embarrassingly confusing times and places. Cf. Plutarch, *Morals* 395 b-d (*The Oracles at Delphi*); Florus, *Epitome of Roman History* 1.32; Isidore, *Etymologies* 16.20.4; Orosius, *Seven Books of History Against the Pagans* 5.3.7. In the *Natural History*, the tale of the Corinthian alloy is used to make a moral point. In ancient times, Pliny explains in *Nat.* 34.5, technique (*ars*) was held in higher esteem (*pretiosior*) than the substance (*materia*) of an artwork; in his time, instead, "though the prices paid for these works of art have grown beyond all limit, the importance attached to this craftsmanship of working in metals has quite disappeared" (*auctoritas artis extincta est*). Not even Chance (*fortuna*), Pliny concludes, is now able to produce art. A close parallel is *Nat.* 35.50 regarding painting and progression to more sophisticated pigments.

37 On Corinthian bronze, see García Morcillo 2010; Darab 2015; Becatti 1951, 13, 162–164, 205–206. See also Isager 1991, 82–83. For the so-called 'livery' bronze, see Jacobson and Weitzman 1995.

38 For example, a first-century CE agate vase, worked to create the impression of figures surfacing from the stone itself (now in Vienna at the Kunsthistorisches Museum, inv. no. X 22; Zwierlein-Diehl 2008, 208–215, 348–349 no. 24). Pliny mentions such an artefact in *Nat.* 37.5, an agate representing Apollo and the Muses, "due not to any artistic intention, but to Nature unaided; and the markings spread in such a way that even the

individual Muses had their appropriate emblems allotted to them". See also Platt 2018b, 258–271.

39 On this anecdote (also in Cicero, *On Divination* 1.23 and 2.48–49), see A. Corso in Pliny–Conte 1982–1988, V, 533, and Catoni 2020. Quintilian (*Institutes of Oratory* 2.19.3) explores the relationship between *materia* and *ars* by engaging with the case study of a block of Parian marble.

40 Cf. *Nat.* 34.49 and 35.54. See A. Corso in Pliny-Conte 1982–1988, V, 345, 347.

41 *DNO*, nos. 2993–3032. Pliny's story about Protogenes' *Ialysus* is discussed in Platt 2016b, 74–76 and 2018b. See also Darab 2012 and 2014a, 216–218; Falaschi 2018.

42 Platt 2018a, 222–225, 235 and 2018c, 497; Carey 2003, 103–104; Darab 2014b, 284–290. See also the commentary in Pliny-Croisille 1985, 212–217.

43 *Nat.* 35.102; see Isager 1991, 130–131.

44 *Nat.* 9.148–150 and 32.123–131. The *Natural History* includes another painting 'completed' by a sponge: the image of a horse by Nealkes, who was unable to represent the animal's foam until he tossed a sponge at the picture (*Nat.* 35.104). This anecdote is also in Plutarch, *Morals* 99 c (*Chance*) and in Valerius Maximus, *Memorable Doings and Sayings* 8.11. *ext.*7 (both without mention of the artist's name), as well as in Dio Chrysostom, *Discourses* 63.4–5 and Sextus Empiricus, *Outlines of Pyrrhonism* 1.28 (both link the incident to Apelles). Stories about chance discoveries made by animals seem to have been popular in antiquity: e.g., the tale about the purple dye, first discovered by Hercules' dog, whose mouth was stained purple from biting into sea snails on the Phoenician coast (Julius Pollux, *Onomasticon* 1.45–49).

45 Naas 2013, 159–163; Wallace-Hadrill 1990, 83.

46 Cf. *Nat.* 2.55. Investigation, in Pliny's view, coincides with the contemplation of Nature; on this concept, which has its roots in the Stoic view of the world, see Beagon 1992, 42–50 and Naas 2012b. For the (fraught) relationship between Nature's project and the human perception of utility, see also Citroni Marchetti 1982.

5 Making art

Illud vero perquam rarum ac memoria dignum est, suprema opera artificum inperfectasque tabulas, sicut Irim Aristidis, Tyndaridas Nicomachi, Mediam Timomachi et quam diximus Venerem Apellis, in maiore admiratione esse quam perfecta, quippe in iis liniamenta reliqua ipsaeque cogitationes artificum spectantur, atque in lenocinio commendationis dolor est manus, cum id ageret, exstinctae.

(*Natural History* 35.145)

In the book on pigments and colours, Pliny mentions four pictures, three by late-Classical masters (Aristides, Nicomachus, and Apelles), and one by an artist from the age of Julius Caesar, Timomachus, as paramount examples of works that became famous owing to their being left unfinished (*inperfectae tabulae*).[1] In particular, Apelles' incomplete depiction of Aphrodite is among very few artworks that are discussed more than once in Pliny's encyclopaedia.[2] Pliny had already presented Apelles' unfinished picture at an earlier point in his treatise (*Nat.* 35.91–92), together with another image of the goddess by the same painter. There, Apelles is credited with two paintings of Aphrodite, both originally displayed at Cos: the famous *Anadyomene* ('rising from the sea') and a later, unfinished, picture.

At *Nat.* 35.91, Pliny explains that Apelles' *Anadyomene* had been brought to Rome and dedicated by Augustus in the temple of his father, Caesar.[3] Unfortunately, the painting had come to bear the signs of age. This intimation of perishability became a powerful indicator of its fine lineage and master's skill (*cessit in gloriam artificis*).[4] In the decades preceding publication of the *Natural History*, however, the state of preservation of the painting had plummeted to the point that Nero ultimately resolved to substitute it with another picture, namely the work of an otherwise-unknown artist, Dorotheus.[5]

DOI: 10.4324/9780429329159-5

On first appearance, the anecdote of Apelles' unfinished Aphrodite constitutes yet another expression of Pliny's interest in artists' lives and his taste for curiosities. Still, it comprises several layers of meaning, due to its participation in a dense network of references throughout the *Natural History*. In the exceptionally lengthy section dedicated to Apelles (*Nat.* 35.79–97), Pliny expands on a number of concepts that are essential to his narrative. Pliny's concern with the status of art and the limits of human ingenuity are concentrated in the anecdotes regarding the unfinished and unrestored (nay, *unrestorable*) images of Aphrodite. The two questions that these incidents elicit are the following. First, what is the relationship between an artwork's value and the elements of craftsmanship, aesthetic merit, and the prestige of tradition? And second, what is the place of integrity and completion—in other words, the elusive concept of *formal perfection*—within the *Natural History*'s ethical and epistemic framework?

Absence and substitution

Pliny's account of Apelles' unfinished picture only becomes clear when one considers what had been said about the painter's complete, more illustrious masterpiece, the *Anadyomene*. The treatment of the *Anadyomene*, in turn, contains compelling analogies with other passages: in particular, Pliny's earlier presentation of another masterpiece in bronze by Lysippus, the statue of Alexander *puer* (*Nat.* 34.63), discussed in Chapter 2. These two stories have parallels with respect to the portrayal of the characters involved, and the criteria undergirding their respective evaluation.

First, both stories are about masters of the late-Classical period, whose work is presented in the *Natural History* as the culmination of Greek art following a long-established tradition. Second, the survival of both Apelles' *Anadyomene* and Lysippus' *Alexander* is threatened by the quintessentially evil emperor, Nero. Confronted with the decay of Apelles' picture, Nero was incapable of (or, indeed, uninterested in) proposing an alternative to its removal and its substitution with a different painting by an obscure artist. The replacement of Apelles' *tabula* seems to be attributed to the emperor's inability to ensure (or, possibly, his disregard for) the preservation of an ancient artwork, rendering the substitutive act one of frustration rather than informed artistic agency. Of course, Nero's choice sits well with what Pliny perceives as the prevailing taste of the time for an 'anonymous art of luxury'. Indeed, Pliny does not mention the subject of Dorotheus' work explicitly, although we may imagine it depicted the goddess Aphrodite like its predecessor. The encyclopaedist simply states that the emperor put another (*alia*), nondescript (i.e., anonymous) picture (*tabula*) in the place of Apelles' masterpiece (*Nat.* 35.91). The verb *substituere*, 'to substitute', which Pliny uses to describe Nero's decision to replace Apelles' *Anadyomene* with a new painting, is rather uncommon in the *Natural History*.[6] The choice of words calls to mind the story about Tiberius' deceitful removal of the *Apoxyomenos* from the Baths of Agrippa, after putting another (anonymous) statue in the place of the stolen masterpiece (*Nat.* 34.62: *alio signo substituto*). Pliny reconstructs Tiberius' and Nero's behaviour through subtle nuances, which do not solely apply to the two emperors' different degrees of reproachable appropriation. While Tiberius is well aware of the excellence of the artwork that he substitutes with another statue (although he is admittedly unprepared for the shared fervour of Roman people for superlative artworks), Nero seems oblivious to the cavernous qualitative gap between a painting by Apelles and one by Dorotheus.

The dynamics of fame functioned similarly in elevating Apelles' second image of Aphrodite, which was left unfinished upon the artist's death, and which ultimately owed its fame to its incompleteness. In both cases, Pliny is explicit about the hand of the master being irreplaceable. As Pliny explains in *Nat.* 35.91–92, it proved impossible to find someone capable of restoring the picture of the *Anadyomene* (*qui reficeret non potuit reperiri*), while with respect to the master's later painting, it could never be completed owing to a lack of artists skilled enough to accomplish Apelles' vision (*nec qui succederet operi ad praescripta liniamenta inventus est*). One picture of Aphrodite owes some of its repute to its unrepaired damages, the other to its status as a perennial work-in-progress. The story of Apelles' paintings of Aphrodite is ultimately one of absence and uniqueness. Owing to either decay or interruption, the two pictures are unified by a status of *inperfectae tabulae*; for both, perfection was neither a matter of simple restitution nor realisation by a different hand.

The choice of finiteness

Pliny's discourse about surfaces intersects with a broader argument regarding artistic integrity and finitude. At *Nat.* 35.145, he argues that works left incomplete upon the death of their creator are sometimes better regarded than finished pieces, largely because they reveal the master's preliminary sketch (*liniamenta*) and thoughts (*cogitationes*).[7] Here, parallels to the earlier presentation of Apelles' two images of Aphrodite are obvious. Key to both sections is the unmistakable and irreplaceable individuality of the artist's sketches (his *praescripta liniamenta*), which other hands fail to follow, thereby constituting the painting's greatest asset.

Pliny mentions other instances of unfinished artworks (owing either to death or exasperation) in Book 35 with regard to the sculptor Arcesilaus (*Nat.* 35.156), a contemporary of Timomachus.[8] Arcesilaus was famous for his preliminary *bozzetti*—which, we may conjecture, were highly regarded by other artists because they incorporated and revealed their maker's creative process—as well as for his unfinished terracotta statues: *Venus Genetrix* for Caesar's Forum and *Felicitas* for Lucius Lucullus.[9] Julius Caesar's association with Venus in the context of the legendary parentage of the *gens* Julia may also be one reason why Augustus displayed the *Anadyomene* by Apelles in the Temple of Caesar.[10] A painting such as the *Anadyomene*, which looked unambiguously ancient, would sit particularly well in a political and artistic program that revolved around the role of origins and the mythical past of Rome.

The problem of finitude constitutes a leitmotif in the books of the *Natural History* dedicated to the visual arts, receiving extensive treatment already in the section on bronze sculpture, in particular with respect to the art of Apollodorus and Callimachus, the two fifth-century BCE artists who had become famous thanks to their disproportionate self-criticism (*Nat.* 34.81 and 34.92).[11] In these passages, Pliny prepares the ground for his penetrating exploration of grace as both an individual quality and a *terminus technicus* of art criticism, which occupies a central position in the section on Apelles. For Pliny (*Nat.* 35.79–81), Apelles' characteristic quality was his awareness of the modes, moments, and significance of artistic processes. This master's merits and doctrine are constructed through a comparison with Protogenes, his rival in the famous challenge of the line and the creator of immensely laborious works (*Nat.* 35.81–83). In Apelles' own words, the grace (χάρις) of his works—which no other artist could match (*sibi neminem parem*)—depended essentially on his innate *simplicitas*, that is, the ability to know "when to take his hand away from a picture" (*Nat.* 35.80: *manum de tabula sciret tollere*).[12] In so doing, he avoided the negative effects of excessive diligence, thereby issuing a perceptive warning against the perils of over-conscientiousness, *nocere saepe nimiam diligentiam*. After all, Apelles was the master of minimalist perfection, whose draughtsmanship was revered as an unparalleled exemplar of *subtilitas* (*Nat.* 35.82).[13] Apelles not only committed to assiduous work—he famously made a point "never to let a day of business to be so fully occupied that he did not practise his art by drawing a line" (*Nat.* 35.84)—but he was expert in judging when to stop working.

Finitude thereby coincides with *gratia*, a quality that pertains to the artist's identity, escapes quantitative assessment, and resists all imitative endeavours.[14] In light of these comments, it becomes clear why, on Pliny's account, the manumission of an artwork's surface (for instance, by means of gilding) would result in the loss of the *gratia artis*, the obliteration of the artist's unique mark, a fate that befell Lysippus' gilded *Alexander*. The idea that even restoration could spoil a work's *gratia* is again explored when Pliny presents a painting by Aristides of Thebes, who is introduced as Apelles' peer, *aequalis eius* (*Nat.* 35.98–100). His picture of a *Tragic Actor with a Boy*, displayed in the Temple of Apollo in Rome, had purportedly forfeited its *gratia* thanks to the incompetence (*inscitia*) of a painter who had been commissioned to clean it (*tergendam*) in preparation for the *Ludi Apollinares*.[15] Clearly, then, any intervention in an artwork, including its maintenance, posed a vital threat to its surface and identity. It is therefore no surprise that Pliny only acknowledges one successful attempt at as delicate a task as restoration. This favourable outcome is conveniently associated with Vespasian, who had entrusted two artists with the repainting of the *Honoris et Virtutis aedes*, Cornelius Pinus and Attius Priscus, who were remarkable for their *auctoritas* (*Nat.* 35.120).[16]

Of course, the public's interest in the unfinished Coan Aphrodite depended, in part, on a grim fascination with its history.[17] Similarly, as perceptively noted by Verity Platt, the effect on today's viewer of the unfinished paintings in the House of the Painters at Work at Pompeii—interrupted by the catastrophic eruption that wiped the town clean off the map in 79 CE—is one of direct, visual intimation of mortality (Figure 5.1).[18] The fate of Apelles' unfinished *Aphrodite* is therefore similar to that of his rival Protogenes' *Ialysus*, brought to completion by a lucky accident (*Nat.* 35.102–103). The success of Apelles' painting too depended on the intriguing happenstance that it should fall to Nature to relieve the artist's hand of completing the work (*Nat.* 35.145: *manus* [...] *exstinctae*), especially considering that Apelles' chief merit was that of knowing instinctually when to do so (*manum de tabula sciret tollere*).[19]

In these passages, the creative act revolves around the interaction between the hand (synecdochical for the body) and its product. The moment when an artwork is finished appears to be determined by concerns regarding *quality* rather than *quantity*, that is, to be judged by the artist's sensibility rather than on account of quantifiable details.[20] To this innate 'bodily' sense for perfection, Nature contributes a certain superordinate force in the creative process, insofar as it is credited for manoeuvring the Aristotelian "instrument of instruments",

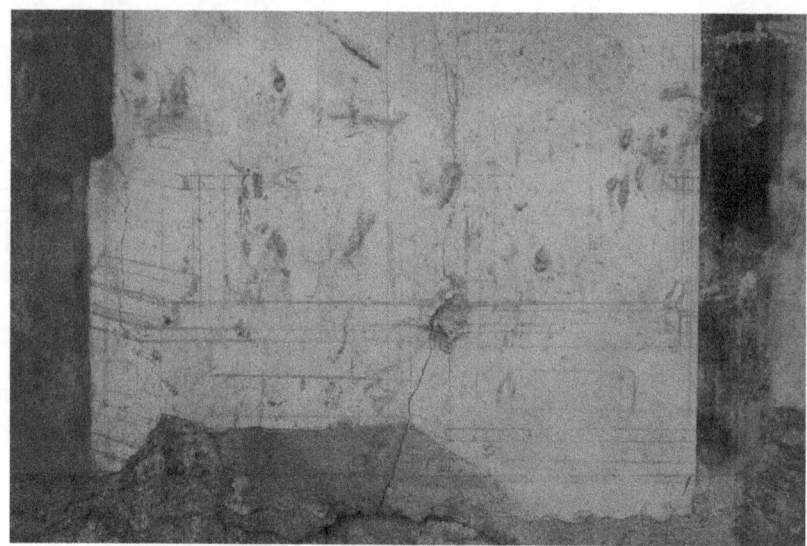

Figure 5.1 Pompeii, House of the Painters at Work (IX 12, 9), room 12, decoration on the East wall, interrupted in 79 CE with preparatory drawings for Fourth-Style architectural views.
Credit: Domenico Esposito.

namely the hand of the artist.[21] In the section about Apelles and his achievements, Pliny constructs a hierarchy of dynamic impulses that participate in artistic production. While, at an earlier point, he introduces the artist's agency as all-important to the physical appearance of artefacts (sc. the irreplaceable hand of Apelles), it is Nature who later emerges as decisive. Indeed, it is Nature whose sensibility for perfection surpasses the plan anticipated through human *liniamenta*.

Perfection, in this framework, remains an elusive quality, insofar as it is utterly individual. According to the *Natural History*, the artist enjoys significant latitude in deciding when to consider a work complete. This argument conspicuously reflects a famous passage from Plato's *Laws* (769a-c), where painting is described as an endlessly incomplete art (οὐδὲν πέρας ἔχειν), until the painter decides that he has reached a point where the picture admits no further improvements.[22] Regardless of where the artist falls on the spectrum of finitude (two painters, such as Protogenes and Apelles, may find themselves at strikingly different points along this line), the question of whether a work is complete rests with him alone. This inextricable link between finitude and individual choice moreover smuggles in a fundamental ambiguity within Plinian aesthetics and a certain tension between a work's conceptual infrastructure and the state of its surfaces. Apelles' unfinished Aphrodite owes most of its fame to its visible *liniamenta*, the preliminary sketches that illuminate the artist's actual thoughts (*cogitationes*). If, however, the artist's project reveals itself mostly in the *liniamenta* of the work, then the irreplaceable dimension of craftsmanship lies rather in the treatment of surfaces, the set of actions and artistic choices that *follow* the first sketch. Apparently no other artist was capable of matching Apelles' prowess for varnishing surfaces, nor could they evince his acute awareness of when to stop working on a picture. Thus, surface values emerge as features that are ultimately impossible to restore, replace, alter, or enhance in any way. Unsurprisingly, it is in the final book of the *Natural History*, which is dedicated to gems and precious stones, and where Nature's deeds are said to triumph over human ingenuity, that these questions become the subject of closer scrutiny and more consistent investigation.

The infinite encyclopaedia

By drawing attention to questions of completeness and integrity, Pliny reconciles the ethical imperative underpinning his account of natural artefacts with the concepts of a broader artistic discourse, as well as with a distinctive interest in individual biographies. The continuation of *inperfecta* (or *inchoata*) *opera* and the restoration of, or tampering with, *perfecta opera* fall under the same reprehensible category of assaults on the intended simplicity of an artist's work.

Significantly, issues related to the process of creation first surface in the *epistula praefatoria*, in which Pliny feels compelled to explain his intellectual program, situating it within a long-standing tradition of learned treatises, and defending the selective criteria of a work that purports to offer "an all-round education". There, he compares his achievements as a collector and organiser of facts to the work of those artists who "used to inscribe their finished works" (*absoluta opera*) with a provisional title such as *Worked on by Apelles* or *Polyclitus* (*Apelles faciebat aut Polyclitus*). This formula stands uncorroborated according to the available evidence of artists' signatures from Greek and Roman antiquity, but nonetheless became, over the centuries, a powerful statement regarding one's confidence, and therefore awareness of place within artistic tradition (Figure 5.2). Through this formula, Pliny constructs art as something that is always in progress (*inchoata*) and never complete (*inperfecta*).[23] By using the imperfect tense to describe a continuous action in the past that may still be in progress, Pliny suggests that artists would be shielded from criticism, implying that they *would* have corrected any remaining mistakes (*velut emendaturo*) had they not been interrupted. The connection to passages about Apelles' unfinished Aphrodite is clear in Pliny's praise for signing artworks as an act of modesty, with every work presented as the artist's latest (*novissima*), "as though they had been snatched away from each of them by fate" (*Praef.* 26–27).

For the purposes of Pliny's encyclopaedia, careful consideration of the author's responsibility and autonomy in choosing contents and

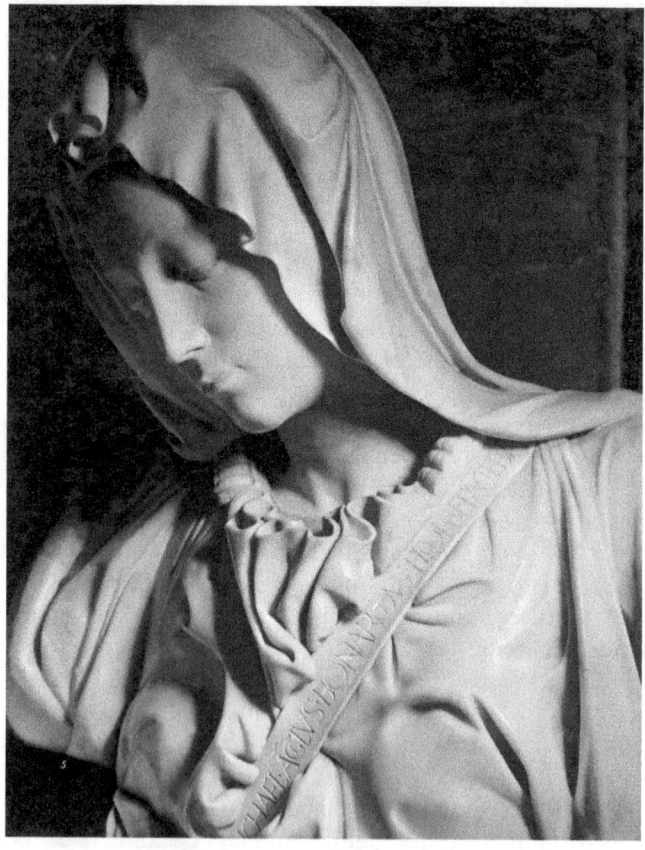

Figure 5.2 Michelangelo Buonarroti, *Pietà*, 1498–1499. Signature *facieba(t)* on the sash across the chest of the Virgin Mary. Città del Vaticano, Basilica di San Pietro.

Credit: AKG / Mondadori.

sources represents a primary concern. Pliny is keenly aware of the challenge posed by his potentially unbounded subject matter, both in terms of the number of items acknowledged and their potential for verification and explanation (*Praef.* 18 and 28). As an intellectual enterprise that is unfinished *per se*, the encyclopaedia rests on a delicate balance between selection, with its implicit corollary of arbitrariness and elective omission, and authority. In its virtually infinite object, the encyclopaedia is a mirror of the world itself, described at the very beginning of the treatise as "finite and resembling the infinite" (*Nat.* 2.2).[24] The parallel between writing the encyclopaedia and the practice of producing, collecting, and viewing artworks is made explicit at other points in the Preface to the *Natural History*, where Pliny compares his work to a storehouse (*thesaurus*), a place for hoarding objects electively preserved owing to their intrinsic significance or historical saliency (*Praef.* 17). The discussion of Apelles' unfinished and unrestored pictures enables Pliny to address questions regarding the burden on artists to decide when their works are complete, while also acknowledging the immensely personal dimension of such a choice. In this sense, the performative aspects of creation not only occupy an essential position in Pliny's presentation of visual art but provide fundamental means for constructing and explaining his view of intellectual work and, more specifically, of his own strategies as a collector of, and writer about, the facts of Nature.

Notes

1 This passage is also discussed from different angles in Platt 2018c; Anguissola 2020. An important article regarding the role and position of unfinished artworks in Roman thought and artistic practice has been published by Massimiliano Papini in 2017. For a discussion of unfinished monuments in the ancient Greek world, see Papini 2019. On the paintings mentioned in *Nat.* 35.145, see the commentary by A. Corso in Pliny-Conte 1982–1988, V, 465 note 2.

2 The unfinished *Aphrodite* and Apelles' painting techniques are also mentioned in two passages by Cicero (*Letters to Friends* 1.9.5, and *Offices* 3.10), who describes the picture's beautifully finished head and bust on an incomplete body. The visual *topos* of a finished head on an unfinished body, which seems to reflect a certain Roman conception of completeness, has enjoyed an extraordinary fortune in later artistic periods; see, e.g., the works collected in the exhibition *Unfinished: Thoughts left Visible* at The Met Breuer in 2016.

3 *DNO*, nos. 2877–2897, 2898–2901. On later interpretations of Pliny's anecdotes about the life of Apelles, see McHam 2013, 47–50.

4 Pliny also plays with the contrast between 'factual disappearance' and 'literary memory', thereby presenting Apelles' picture as eclipsed by age and

yet made famous by the Greek verses that sing its praises. I here follow C. Mayhoff's text (*versibus Graecis tantopere dum laudatur, aevis victa, sed inlustrata*). Most translators and commentators instead prefer to read the passage as *versibus Graecis tali opere, dum laudatur, victo sed inlustrato*, see Pliny-Rackham 1961, 329: "this like other works is eclipsed yet made famous by the Greek verses which sing its praises"; Pliny-Jex-Blake, Sellers 1896, 127: "being, like other works of the kind, at once eclipsed yet rendered famous by the Greek epigrams written in her praise"; Pliny-Croisille 1985, 74: "ce chef-d'œuvre fut surpassé par les poètes grecs don't il reçut les éloges, mais n'en fut pas moins ainsi rendu célèbre"; Pliny-Conte 1982–1988, V, 388: "un'opera esaltata in versi greci che hanno sì superato in valore il quadro stesso, ma lo hanno anche reso celebre"; Pliny-Ferri 2000, 207: "i versi greci hanno certamente superato il quadro colle loro lodi, però al tempo stesso lo hanno reso celebre"; Pliny-König, Winkler 2007, 75 (and 307): "ein solch bedeutendes Werk durch das Lob in griechischen Versen in den Schatten gestellt, aber auch berühmt gemacht wurde". S. Ferri (Pliny-Ferri 2000, 106) remarks that "il concetto di *victo sed inlustrato* è pliniano" and points to a parallel in *Nat.* 34.57. There is a famous tradition of epigrams also for the *Medea* by Timomachus, cited among unfinished works like Apelles' last picture of Aphrodite; see Gutzwiller 2004; Platt 2018c, 503–510.

5 On Dorotheus, see A. Corso in Pliny-Conte 1982–1988, V, 389, 891.

6 Throughout the *Natural History*, *substituere* appears only eight times (also in *Nat.* 5.50, 5.117, 8.184, 10.151, 12.118, 18.17), mostly with a neutral meaning and occasionally referring to actions of selfish deceit.

7 On the meaning of *liniamenta* and *cogitationes*, see Papini 2017, 45; Pollitt 1974, 392–297; Daneu Lattanzi 1982, 99–100. Pliny-Ferri 2000, 207–209, 249 translates *liniamenta* as "abbozzo già disegnato" and "rimanenti parti abbozzate". In his commentary to *Nat.* 35.145, Ferri explains *liniamenta* as "le linee di contorno, il disegno preliminare", *reliquia* as "linee superstiti del disegno originario, in quanto non sono ancora sparite, assorbite dal colore", and *cogitationes* as "dubbi, incertezze, tentativi, progetti, non certo il concetto o fantasma dell'autore nel senso moderno". See also Pliny-Croisille 1985, 98: "les traces de l'esquisse et la conception même de l'artiste" (also *ibid.*, 139 par. 15 note 3, 153–154 par. 145 notes 8, 9); R. Mugellesi in Pliny-Conte 1982–1988, V, 463 ("linee del progetto"); Pliny-Rackham 1961, 367 ("preliminary drawings"); Pliny-König, Winkler 2007, 111 ("die zurückgelassenen Skizzen" and "die Überlegungen der Künstler"). Pliny also uses the word *liniamenta* to describe the guidelines that artists sought in Polyclitus' *Canon, veluti a lege quadam*.

8 In *Nat.* 36.124, Pliny discusses an example of unfinished infrastructure, the drainage channel at Lake Fucinus planned by emperor Claudius, which his "malicious successor" Nero left incomplete.

9 Caesar seems to have been particularly interested in 'unfinished works' (or, perhaps, uninterested in finitude as an 'objective quality'), see *Nat.* 35.136, 145, 156. On Caesar's programmatic presentation of Greek artworks in the *Forum Iulium*, see Rutledge 2012, 226–235; Bravi 2012, 77–82 and 2014, 85–95.

10 Rutledge 2012, 234; Bravi 2012, 100–102 and 2014, 118–121. On Augustus' exploitation of the Trojan myth, see Erskine 2001, 15–23, 234–235,

255–256. For the Temple of Caesar and, in general, on Julius Caesar's role in Augustan Rome, see White 1988; Favro 1996, 95–98.

11 On Pliny's concept of perfection in the field of the figural arts, see also Duarte 2009.

12 On χάρις/*gratia*, see Pollitt 1974, 297–301, 380–381; Moussy 1966, 407–435. For the use of Greek words in the *Natural History*, see the comments in Chapter 3 with earlier literature.

13 On *subtilitas* and the ability to understand an artwork's limits, see Michel 1987, 58; Pigeaud 1987, 103–106. The discussion on unfinished artworks encourages following M. Merleau-Ponty (2007, esp. 371–373) in challenging the "prosaic conception of the line as a positive attribute and property of the object in itself" and acknowledging the tension between visible and invisible, positive and negative materialised by the line.

14 For Pliny's treatment of imitation, see Chapter 3, as well as Anguissola 2006 and 2012, 79–87.

15 *DNO*, nos. 2746–2747. According to the commentary by A. Corso in Pliny-Conte 1982–1988, V, 399 note 1, the restoration had been commissioned by Marcus Junius Silanus for the *Ludi* in 13 BCE.

16 A. Corso in Pliny-Conte 1982–1988, V, 911, 916. On the Flavian emperors' engagement with the artistic and monumental landscape of Rome, see Chapter 6. Vespasian may have also played a role in the survival of the *Anadyomene*, at least if we accept that Suetonius is referring to this painting when he states that Vespasian generously rewarded artists such as the restorer (*refector*) of the Venus of Cos and the Colossus of Nero (*Vespasian* 18). However, owing to textual issues with this passage, it cannot be ruled out that Suetonius refers here to the statue of Venus *quam Vespasianus imperator in operibus Pacis suae dicavit antiquorum dignam fama* (*Nat.* 36.27), see Anguissola 2012, 168 note 104.

17 On the role of chance in the determination of an artwork's prestige (*auctoritas*), see Robert 1995, esp. 296.

18 Platt 2018c, 499. On the House of the Painters at Work (IX 12, 9), see Varone and Béarat 1997; Esposito 2016, 174–176 and 2017, 268–271.

19 The idea of a work-in-progress, which has been interrupted, is highlighted by the form *cum id ageret*, as noted by Platt 2018c, 496; cf. *Nat.* 36.31 for the passage about the Mausoleum of Halicarnassus, which presents textual parallels in both the use of the verb *agere* and the insistence on the concept of the artist's *hand*. It seems no coincidence that in the case of the *Anadyomene* the relationship of the new picture with the painter Dorotheus is stressed by referring to his *manus*. In Pliny's presentation, each one of the paintings mentioned in this section (Apelles' *Anadyomene*, the unfinished Aphrodite, Dorotheus' "other image") is inextricably connected to the physical presence of its maker.

20 Pliny, immediately before the section in Book 36 about the work of unknown or hardly distinguishable craftsmen (*Nat.* 36.27–38), presents the artist's *manus* as a characteristic feature which enables viewers to determine an artwork's paternity (*Nat.* 36.26). On the role of an artist's hand in theories of embodiment (especially as applied to ancient Greek and Roman art), see the excellent introduction by Gaifman and Platt 2018. In Book 36, Pliny uses the metaphor of the hand in describing the properties of a magnet, a substance which seems to blur the distinction between

animated bodies and inanimate matter, endowed by Nature with "senses and hands" (*Nat.* 36.126).

21 Aristotle, *On the Soul* 432a1–3 (and *Parts of Animals* 687a10). According to Aristotle, ἡ χεὶρ ὄργανόν ἐστιν ὀργάνων because it can utilise any other instrument, thereby enabling them to be instruments in the first place, see Polansky 2010, 496.

22 For this passage and its relationship to Pliny's concept of finitude, see Citroni Marchetti 2011, 48–53.

23 See Citroni Marchetti 2011, 48; Naas 2002, 54–57; see also Platt 2018c, 496–497. On the modern reception of this passage, and the tradition of 'Plinian' signatures with the verb *faciebat*, see McHam 2013, 183–203; Hegener 2013; Goffen 2001, spec. 319–328. Wang 2004 argues that Michelangelo's choice to sign as *facieba(t)*, without the final 't', may indeed be a pun on the very meaning of *faciebat* and the imperfect tense. On *absolutus, consummatus, perfectus* in the Latin discourse on the figural arts, see Pollitt 1974, 301–303, 336–339, 416–422.

24 See Carey 2003, 30–32.

6 Looking at art

Romae quidem multitudo operum et iam obliteratio ac magis officiorum negotiorumque acervi omnes a contemplatione tamen abducunt,
quoniam otiosorum et in magno loci silentio talis admiratio est. Qua
de causa ignoratur artifex eius quoque Veneris, quam Vespasianus
imperator in operibus Pacis suae dicavit antiquorum dignam fama.

(*Natural History* 36.27)

The narrative in Book 36 is organised into several self-contained
sections: sculpture, various types of marble and the technologies for
cutting slabs, impressive monuments of stone in other parts of the
world, the 'marvels' of Rome, stones with medicinal uses, construction
stones, mosaic floors, glass and obsidian, and fire.[1] Pliny concludes
with the legendary origins of the *Compitalia* festivals, dedicated to 'the
deities of the crossroads'. Pliny's movements between one topic and the
next are orchestrated according to a variety of associations, not least
materials, size, geography, technical challenges, and ethical worries
concerning certain moral oppositions, particularly between modesty
and *luxuria*, tied to discussions of the public and private spheres.

Around the text's midpoint we find one of the best-known paragraphs of the entire *Natural History* (*Nat.* 36.101), which sets the tone
for the foregoing presentation, shifting the discourse towards the marvels (*miracula*) of Rome. Pliny imagines these monuments gathered
together onto a great heap (*universitate vero acervata et in quendam
unum cumulum coiecta*), one that is so massive that it would look like
an alternate world concentrated in a single place (*non alia magnitudo
exurget quam si mundus alius quidam in uno loco*).[2] After many volumes
discussing 'all' the things and facts of Nature, Pliny finally engages
with the place, people, and institutions that he sees controlling the
world's resources. The ensuing description of sewers and aqueducts

DOI: 10.4324/9780429329159-6

highlights the difference between the Roman pursuit of *utilitas*—albeit jeopardised by questionable developments in matters of taste and ostentation—and the idle creations of foreign rulers.[3] The passage quoted at the beginning of this chapter provides the key to understanding Pliny's vision of Rome as both the centre of an empire and a living, urban organism. There, Pliny develops his argument regarding the conflict between *growth* and *loss* which is integral to Roman expansion.[4] The accumulation of marvels (*acervata*) went hand-in-hand with the proliferation of official and business duties (*officiorum negotiorumque acervi*), which took a toll on the human ability to perceive, make sense of, and *remember* art.[5]

This chapter explores questions regarding the modes and circumstances of artistic spectatorship, as well as the ways in which Pliny understood the role of art within Rome's urban fabric. Questions include how artworks should be viewed and appreciated, in terms of both their display context and the viewer's state of mind. Finally and of primary importance for understanding the place of 'art history' within Pliny's encyclopaedia: how do matters of attention and memory inform Pliny's argument that Rome is the paradigmatic political, living city, and, as such, a *locus* of social interaction?

The leisure of attention

Pliny's account of the accumulation of images seems to reflect the historical reality of imperial Rome. At the same time, his acknowledgment of Rome's landscape (even its detrimental aspects) follows his 'periegetical approach' to marble sculpture, as based on personal, first-hand experience.[6] On the one hand, stressing the role of the urban landscape in contributing to ignorance about many exquisite marble artworks is an ingenious strategy on Pliny's part and helps to exonerate the relative shortness of this section compared to those on bronze sculpture and painting. On the other hand, this passage provides important insights regarding the context and circumstances for viewing sculpture, suggesting an awareness of statuary as an urban phenomenon, which entailed shared practices, responses, and challenges.[7]

The comprehension and appreciation of art requires freedom from public duties (the sphere of *officium* and *negotium*), as well as the possibility for leisurely immersing oneself in intellectual contemplation. *Otium*, 'quiet', is a premise for the *contemplatio* which, in turn, provokes *admiratio* and thus helps to reinforce the remembrance of objects and their biographies.[8] The fundamental antithesis between *negotium* and *otium*, and its impact on intellectual activities, emerges at several points in the Preface, where Pliny details his work's concept and program. There (*Praef.* 6), he establishes an opposition between the superior competence and higher duties of his work's dedicatee, the future emperor Titus, and the "humble people" to whom his treatise is aimed, "the mob of farmers and artisans, and after them those who can devote themselves leisurely to their studies" (*studiorum otiosi*).[9] Pliny, in one sentence, commingles the whole spectrum of Roman society—and of Titus' subjects—beginning with the humble multitude "who made this empire great", relinquishing their plough and hearth (cf. *Nat.* 36.111) and then including the *actual*, prospective readers of the encyclopaedia: those sophisticates who are in a position to pursue their intellectual curiosity.[10] At a later point in the *epistula praefatoria*, Pliny returns to the ideal conditions for intellectual activities, present-ing himself as a man beset with duties (*occupati officiis*) and explaining that his work had been composed across a few (largely nocturnal) mo-ments of rest (*Praef.* 18).[11]

Intellectual pursuits therefore depend upon certain conditions regard-ing time and place: spare time and deep silence in one's surroundings. Pliny's imagined reader, as well as the ideal spectator of Rome's art-works, belongs to a category defined by time: *otiosi*, men (temporarily) relieved of their commitments who are interested in the dedicated study of vast amounts of both written (the encyclopaedia) and visual (the artis-tic heritage of Rome) information. The need for public spaces designed for silent contemplation is reiterated in the narrative about the collection of Asinius Pollio, a prominent figure of the late-Republican and Augus-tan period. Pliny introduces Pollio's collection as his *monumenta*, mean-ing both the statues he owned and the physical space in which they were displayed (*Nat.* 36.33).[12] Indeed, being an "ardent enthusiast" (*acris vehe-mentiae*), Pollio wished for his artworks to be examined with the utmost attention (*sic quoque spectari monumenta sua voluit*). His choice to organ-ise his marble sculptures in a dedicated space corrresponded with his desire for a place where he could 'examine' each piece in an environment suitable for *contemplatio*.[13] After all, Pollio had retired from Rome's po-litical life in 39/38 BCE just after his triumph over the Parthini, a tribe from the province of Illyricum, and dedicated the rest of his life to intel-lectual *otium* and artistic patronage.[14]

The intensity of gaze

Comments regarding the importance of 'concentration' may largely depend upon Pliny's late-Republican sources and his own interest in the 'museum-like enjoyment' of art.[15] This perspective emerges in a small number of passages scattered throughout the final books of the *Natural History*, which insist on the preference for frontal, eye-level viewing.[16] Immediately after the section about the production of individual marble sculptures by multiple artists, which raises the issue of 'problematic attribution', Pliny praises Diogenes, a first-century BCE sculptor from Athens, for his caryatids, placed between the columns of Agrippa's Pantheon (*Nat.* 36.38), as well as for his acroterial figures, which are less well known owing to their elevation (*propter altitudinem loci minus celebrata*).[17] The possibility that statues on a temple's roof would escape attention—unlike those 'framed' between columns—aligns with an ancient commonplace about sight, as derived from the Stoic theory of perception. The idea that distance, given that it stretches the visual flux over an excessive interval of space, may produce a qualitative degradation of sight is widespread in Latin literary sources.[18] For instance, Vitruvius calls upon the Stoic concept of 'haptic sight' in making the case that temple lintels should be made larger than necessary in order to compensate for progressive stretching of vision and perceived reduction in size.[19]

Pliny's interest in the museum-like display of artworks is not exclusive to marble sculpture. This is clear from a group of passages about painted plaster from Book 35. There, Pliny blames Caligula's behaviour on two pictures of Helena and Atalanta at Lanuvium, which had spiked his lust to such an extent that he tried (unsuccessfully) to tear them from the wall.[20] By referring to the emperor's uncontrolled lust (*Nat.* 35.18: *libidine accensus*) and implying that the paintings' removal served the mere purpose of private enjoyment, Pliny casts a negative light on the removal of the figural parts of wall paintings, which he elsewhere describes in positive terms. The occasional removal of decorative features from ancient buildings (which later find themselves enclosed in frames) can, in some cases, form part of an entirely honourable process of maintenance (*Nat.* 35.154). On Varro's account, when the *aedes* of Ceres near the Circus Maximus underwent restoration following a fire, the clay acroterial figures (by the early fifth-century BCE masters Damophilus and Gorgasus) were lost, perhaps because their placement commanded little visual attention, leading to their relative lack of protection. However, their paintings on terracotta slabs were excised from the wall, finding their way into frames for posterity (*crustas parietum excisas tabulis marginatis inclusas*).[21] This passage emphasises the contrast between the dispersion and hoarding of two disparate classes of material.

Later in the narrative (*Nat.* 35.173), Pliny mentions the removal (*excisum*) from walls at Sparta of certain exceptional pieces of painted plasterwork, which were later framed (*ligneis formis inclusum*) and shipped to Rome for placement in the Comitium. Notwithstanding the quality of the work, Pliny points out that what impressed the Roman public most was the technical skill involved in the removal. This anecdote is taken from Vitruvius, who also refers to the incident of the *picturae excisae* and *inclusae in ligneis formis* from Sparta in his volume about the materials used in architecture (*On Architecture* 2.8.9), albeit without commenting further on the pictures' quality and appreciation in Rome.[22] Unlike the paintings from the *aedes* of Ceres, which had to be rescued following a fire, the images from Sparta were chosen owing to their quality alone, isolated as fragments and included in a new context as both valuable *ornamenta* and the tangible sign of Rome's imperial prowess.[23] Pliny's interest in the *picturae excisae* may reflect a taste for the inclusion of figural tables into decorated walls, a practice that seems to have been widespread around the mid- to late-first century CE. On the painted walls of Pompeii and Herculaneum, numerous thin recesses, now devoid of content, may have been occupied by *picturae ligneis formis inclusae*.[24] One such picture, depicting winged Cupids at work, was found in House V, 17–18 at Herculaneum (Figure 6.1). The painting was created on a thin layer of *tectorium* in

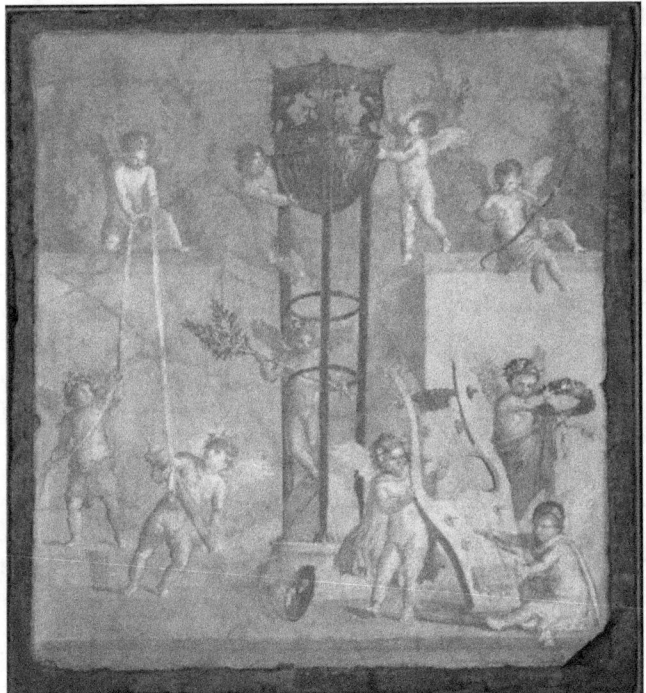

Figure 6.1   Fresco panel in a wooden frame, depicting winged Cupids at work, from House V, 17–18 at Herculaneum. 102.5 × 94 cm. Herculaneum, Parco Archeologico, no. 77872.

Credit: Herculaneum, Parco Archeologico.

the artist's studio, employing the fresco technique. Once finished, the work was enclosed in a wooden frame and then included in a recess in the Fourth-Style wall.

A profound difference, however, exists between the fragmentary paintings from Sparta and the framed plasterwork from the Vesuvian sites: the former had been removed from their original context, while the latter participates in a decorative strategy of *mise en abyme* and had been produced as part of their Roman, domestic environment (as an *artificial fragment*). Nevertheless, in both cases the more or less conspicuous presence of a frame must have succeeded in isolating the image from its surroundings. As Georg Simmel suggests in his now-classic treatment of frames, the frame highlights the remoteness and difference of the artwork from the sphere of actual life.[25] Frames reinforce the 'detached gaze' that pictorial spectatorship invites, determining the boundaries within which viewers should focus their *contemplatio*, thereby regulating the time employed in acknowledging, making sense of, and familiarising oneself with an image.[26] Provided that the admiration of art—and the memory of artists and artworks—depends upon the availability of spare time among *officia* and *negotia*, it becomes clear why museum-like displays serve to assist overtaxed Romans in deciding when enough information about a certain work has been acquired and consolidated.

Concentration as power

Two key differences between Vitruvius' and Pliny's account of the painted plaster brought to Rome from Sparta are the latter's insistence on the works' beauty and the challenges involved in their removal. This remark sits well with Pliny's fascination with technical innovations, and, in particular, with moving objects and building materials. Unsurprisingly, in Book 36, where the presentation of marble sculpture follows conspicuously 'periegetic' criteria and culminates in the famous comparison between the world's and Rome's marvels, the achievements connected with transportation (to Rome, of course) occupy a central place.[27] While the book opens with predictable negative comments about man's mangling of the natural landscape, the very same feats of engineering become the objects of praise when it comes to describing the capital of the empire.[28]

The key to understanding Pliny's ambivalent construction of Rome's 'artistic overcrowding' (*multitudo operum* at *Nat.* 36.27 and *miracula* [...] *acervata* at *Nat.* 36.101) lies in the *Natural History*'s moralising account of art and, in particular, in the tension between private appropriation and public enjoyment.[29] In a famous passage from Book 35 (*Nat.* 35.26), Pliny refers to a lofty speech delivered by Agrippa, in which Augustus' right-hand man and son-in-law advocated for the public display of artworks, thereby decrying their 'banishment' to private country houses (*in villarum exilia pelli*).[30] In its intimation of movement, the choice of words is reminiscent of the passages regarding Tiberius' and Nero's abscission of artworks from the public sphere (*Nat.* 34.62, 34.84, 35.70). All of these examples play with the idea of artworks being bandied around and held captive, either by removing them from the city—the place of *negotium*—to the countryside—the purlieu *par excellence* of *otium*—or by concentrating them in the secluded spaces of one's urban house (albeit one, such as Nero's *Domus Aurea*, which is explicitly presented as larger than any country estate). The story of the *Apoxyomenos*, being first removed and then returned, seems to fit in that 'cycle of withdrawal and return' that has been observed in reading Suetonius' *Life of Tiberius* through the lense of proxemic communication strategies.[31] In this sense, Pliny organises his anecdotes about artworks' removal and displacement with a view to emphasising *spatial* relationships, in particular their interruption and modification.

Whereas Tiberius is depicted as an insatiable collector, doting on his masterpieces in the impenetrable privacy of his *cubiculum*, Nero's entire residence (the *Domus Aurea*) is presented as a veritable prison for artworks, especially those by the Roman painter Famulus (*Nat.* 35.120: *carcer eius artis*).[32] Pliny thus includes among other captives not only individual objects but also abstract qualities such as someone's *ars*. When referring to the interior spaces of the *Domus Aurea*, in which the emperor stockpiled his looted artistic wares (*Nat.* 34.84 and 36.111), Pliny consistently chooses the word *sellarium* ('private parlour', 'boudoir'), a rather uncommon term that occurs nowhere else in the encyclopaedia, and which Suetonius employs in similar circumstances.[33] Both of these passages illuminate Pliny's use of anecdotes about moving artworks, as well as the antithesis between public and private, *negotium* and *otium*—contrasts that are indispensable to the construction of his historical narrative, as well as his perspective of present-day Rome. While the *Natural History* does not necessarily present the removal of artworks to Rome negatively, in the case of Nero the author stresses the violence of the removal, while remaining silent on any engineering feats that may have been accomplished thereby.[34] It is clear that Pliny's criticism concerns the *destination* and *function* of the looted artwork, not the mere fact of their being brought to Rome. In Book 36, following a digression about ostentation and wastefulness in the domestic sphere,[35] Pliny refers to Nero's *sellaria* again to exemplify the emperor's subversion of *mores* and acceptable practices—his smaller, private rooms being larger than the cultivated fields of the humble farmers who had laid the very foundations of the Roman state.[36] Nero's outsized boudoirs loom over the city of Rome, encircling it as an avaricious, menacing border (*urbem totam cingi* in *Nat.* 36.111).[37] Implicitly, the reversal of natural and man-made landscapes—recreating the countryside (*rus*) in the heart of the monumental city (*urbs*)—disturbs the 'correct' enjoyment of intellectual *otium*, which should take place in one's spare time, in dedicated locations instead of supplanting business altogether.

Pliny dwells on the consequences of Nero's demise, including the dismantling of the *Domus Aurea*, wiped out together with the memory of its decorator. This perspective becomes clearer through Pliny's direct contrast of the loss of Famulus' 'captive art' with the fame enjoyed by two other Roman painters of his time, Cornelius Pinus and Attius Priscus, who worked for Vespasian on the restoration of the Temple of Honour and Virtue. While one's art was imprisoned inside Nero's palace, the others' shone in the Flavian emperors' program of public magnificence. Vespasian's public program, which entailed the redeployment of pieces formerly 'hidden' in the *Domus Aurea* within the new *Templum Pacis* (*Nat.* 34.84), replaced the memory of Nero's private extravaganza.[38]

Pliny's discussion of Rome's anonymous mass of statues cited at the incipit of this chapter kicks off a lengthy section on the most notable marbles on display in Rome.[39] After mentioning the statue of Aphrodite carved by Praxiteles, "which made Cnidus a famous city" (*Nat.* 36.20–21), Pliny refers to a naked statue of the same goddess by another fourth-century BCE sculptor, Scopas (*Nat.* 36.26), which had been placed in the temple built by Brutus Callaecus (consul, 138 BCE) near the Circus Flaminius. Surpassing even the masterpiece by Praxiteles, Scopas' statue would have made any other place but Rome famous (*quemcumque alium locum nobilitatura*). The presentation of the achievements of Classical and late-Classical masters ends with a reference to Rome—the place towards which everything else converges, becoming part of a 'heap of marvels'. The following paragraph complains about the minimal availability of moments and places designed for silent contemplation and the construction of memory, to the point that even a (third) statue of Aphrodite/Venus—capable of rivalling those by the ancient masters—standing in the new monumental heart of Rome (the *Templum Pacis*) remained authorless.

In the *Natural History*, the *Templum Pacis* functions as a kind of 'monumental equivalent' to the encyclopaedia.[40] There, in the words of the roughly contemporaneous Flavius Josephus, "all (πάντα) the rarities were collected", which men could previously only admire by traversing vast swathes of the inhabited world (περὶ πᾶσαν [...] τὴν οἰκουμένην), encountering them "one after the other" (ἄλλο παρ' ἄλλοις).[41] By integrating them into his forum as a civic asset, Vespasian had effectively endowed Nero's possessions (and many other previously dispersed artworks) with renewed significance. For now they evidenced Rome's new political course, showcasing the reach of its empire, as well as the stability of Flavian power. The idea of 'collecting as a monument to peace' is reinforced by the peculiar arrangement of the building. Long strips, which are clearly visible on the Severan marble map of Rome (Figure 6.2), ran parallel through the vast open space enclosed in the precinct. Previously interpreted as beds for plants and flowers, these rectilinear features are now thought to be canals and basins, part of elaborate waterworks.[42] In light of the uncertainties that

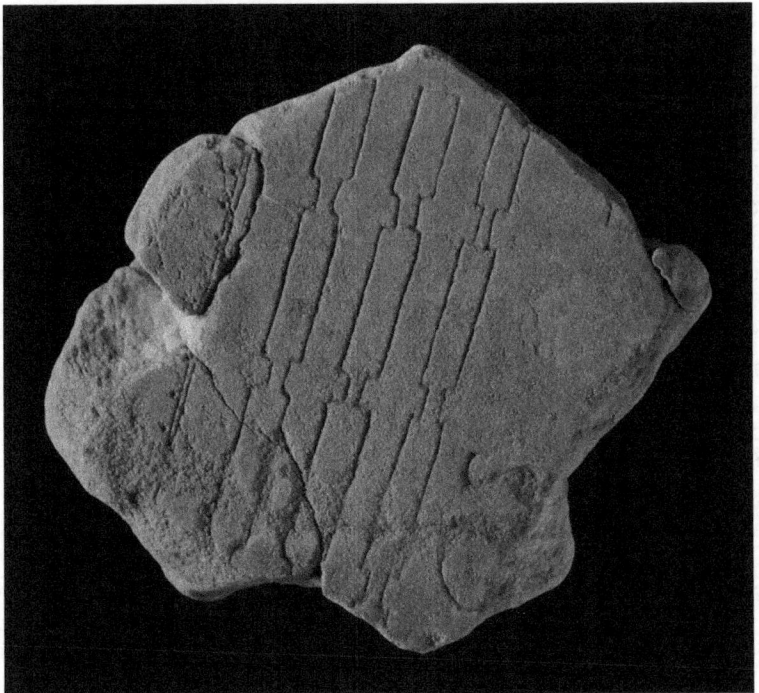

Figure 6.2 Fragment 15c of the Severan Marble Plan of Rome (*Forma Urbis Romae*), depicting a portion of Vespasian's *Templum Pacis*. Rome, Museo della Civiltà Romana.

Credit: Rome, Sovrintendenza Capitolina ai Beni Culturali (Stanford Digital Forma Urbis Romae Project).

still affect the reconstruction of the large courtyard, it seems inappropriate to suggest that the building hosted an actual 'botanical collection', signifying Rome's global control over nature.[43] It is nonetheless possible that the channels were flanked by tidy rows of shrubs, hedges, or flowers. Indeed, it has been conjectured that raised flower beds may have been placed over the water conduits, which were perhaps used for irrigation.[44] In any case, the large, enclosed space, dominated by water and plants, must have created a strikingly different environment from the busy streets and squares at the heart of Rome. The longitudinal features organised movement in the courtyard along a series of repetitive rectilinear paths, enabling leisurely perambulation that was conducive to calm and concentration.[45] By bringing an accessible, methodically arranged adaptation of the natural world into the centre of Rome, the *Templum Pacis* provided the ideal atmosphere for *otium*, understood as an intellectual break from the pressures of official and business duties.

The narrative of art, in Pliny's account, is one of progressive *concentration*, which is organised into concentric circles: the objects gathered in Rome, as displayed in public buildings, encouraged leisured admiration, having been carefully curated to sit in the immediate visual field of the observer. While the natural world is often depicted in the *Natural History* as a sequence of distinctive environments, which 'replicate' the same basic dynamics, the city of Rome offers all the variety of an 'alternative world' (*Nat.* 36.101), collected as if overlapping in multiple layers "in one single place".[46] Pliny's insistence on 'concentrated accessibility' and 'gaze' culiminates in the opening of the last volume on gems. There, Nature's grandeur is concentrated in the smallest of objects to such a point that a single gemstone may alone constitute the supreme paradigm of Nature's potential. Implicitly, the concentration and reduction at work here parallels Pliny's very writing of the encyclopaedia, which involved balancing the preservation of a large body of knowledge—threatened by the distractions of modern life—with uncompromising selection criteria.

Notes

1 Pliny-Conte 1982–1988, V, 512–514; Pliny-André, Bloch, Rouveret 1981, 7–19; Isager 1991, 206–211.
2 Pliny mentions Rome's 'concentrated' landscape also at *Nat.* 3.67 (on the density and elevation of Rome's buildings); see Carey 2003, 45–46. In *Nat.* 3.39–40 Pliny introduces Italy as "a land which is at once the nursling and the mother of all other lands", referring to the coast of Campania as a unique place (*uno in loco*) where Nature has concentrated her efforts;

see also *Nat.* 12.12 and 37.201–202. On Pliny's relationship to the literary tradition of *laudes Italiae*, see Zehnacker 1987; Segenni 2000; Naas 2002, 233–234, 313–315, 427–432, 449–460; Bispham 2007. On Pliny's construction of Rome's landscape as mirroring a tension between 'peripheries' and 'centre' in the treatise's ideology, see Naas 2011a. For a discussion of the strategies and cultural assumptions behind the ancient praises of cities, see Pernot 1993, 178–216.

3 *Nat.* 36.75. See Naas 2002, 327–352, 371–376, 378–381, 387–390; 2004; 2011a.

4 This paragraph introduces a section on anonymous artists (*Nat.* 36.27–29), followed by a discussion of artworks made by multiple artists, whose individual contribution is scarcely noticeable (*Nat.* 36.30–38).

5 Forms of the verb *acervo* (or related terms, such as the adverb *acervatim*) do not occur elsewhere in Pliny's Books 33–37; for other instances, see the Index to Book 2 and *Nat.* 4.69; see Carey 2003, 82, 99–100. Both *Nat.* 36.27 and 36.101 stress the concept of a remarkable 'quantity' or 'size' (*multitudo, magnitudo*); in *Nat.* 36.27, *magnitudo* is attested in place of *multitudo* in several manuscript copies (Pliny-Mayhoff 1875–1906, V [1986, first ed. 1897], 315; Pliny-Eichholz 1962, 20; Pliny-André, Bloch, Rouveret 1981, 57). The idea of *magnitudo* as an obstacle to retaining memory is made explicit in *Nat.* 24.5.

6 Pliny's *Index auctorum* suggests that he was familiar with a number of technical treatises *de pictura* (*On Painting*) and *de toreutice* (*On Bronze Statuary*), while lacking comparable references for marble. As observed by Settis 1999, 41–42, 44, this may have encouraged him to develop new strategies for the presentation of artworks. For the prevailing preference for marble statues in Pliny's times, see Isager 1991, 148–149, 175–177. In a passage from Book 34 (*Nat.* 34.35), Pliny notes the proliferation of bronze statues, albeit in different terms, as a disclaimer regarding the impossibility of treating the subject fully.

7 Stewart 2003, 119–156 addresses the question of whether the Romans perceived statues as a *collective* class of objects or as a 'population'. This attitude is clear in a later source from the early sixth century CE, Cassiodorus' *Formula*, which was addressed to the urban prefect, calling for the establishment of an architect for the city of Rome (*Variae* 7.15). In this heartfelt plea, he describes the statues of Rome as "a population [...] almost equal to that created by nature". On the imagery of Rome's population of statues, "as cosmopolitan as its human population", see Edwards 2003.

8 *Otiosi* in *Nat.* 36.27 is translated as "(being at) leisure" by Pliny-Eichholz 1962, 21, and as "die Muße haben" in Pliny-König, Hopp 2007, 29. R. Bloch in Pliny-André, Bloch, Rouveret 1981, 56 understands *otium* as "oisiveté" ('idleness'), highlighting the *temporal* dimension of *otium*. R. Mugellesi (in Pliny-Conte 1982–1988, V, 561) instead translates Pliny's expression as "tranquilli", stressing the state of inner peace required for artistic spectatorship; see the comments in Poggio 2018, 192–193.

9 For an excellent discussion of the problems related to the translation of *studiorum otiosi*, see Naas 2002, 46–51. See G. Ranucci in Pliny-Conte 1982–1988, I (1982), 7 ("chi studia solo a tempo perso"); J. Beaujeu (Les Belles Lettres, Collection Budé, 1950), 49 ("enfin à occuper des loisirs

studieux"); Carey 2003, 15 ("those with enough time to devote themselves to study"); Citroni Marchetti 2005b, 43 ("chi ha tempo da dedicare agli studi"); Nikitinski 1998, 346 ("solche, die [freie] Zeit für gelehrte Studien haben" and "Dilettanten"). H. Rackham in the Loeb Classical Library edition translates this expression with a negative meaning (*Natural History*, I, 1967, 7: "students who have nothing else to occupy their time", also accepted by Schulz 2019, 349), as do R. König and G. Winkler in their *Sammlung Tusculum* German translation, albeit in a different sense, stressing the especially *intellectual* pursuits of the *otiosi* (*Naturkunde. Lateinisch-deutsch. Buch I*, 1997, 9: "solche, die sich für höhere Studien keine Zeit nehmen").

10 For Pliny's 'ideal' or 'intended reader', see G.B. Conte in Pliny-Conte 1982–1988, I (1982), XXXVI; Citroni Marchetti 1991, 15–18, 75; 2005a, 108–109; 2005b; 2011, 22, 44–45; Isager 1991, 23–31 and 2006b, 115–116; Nikitinski 1998; Naas 2002, 51–53; Morello 2011.

11 Citroni Marchetti 1991, 18–19 and 2011, 21, 32–33, 37–43; Isager 1991, 225–228; Healy 1999, 26–27. On the rhetoric of nocturnal writing, see Ker 2004. For the concept of *otium* in the Republican and Augustan periods, see André 1966.

12 For Asinius Pollio's collection (*Nat.* 35.10, 36.23, 24, 25, 33–34), see Becatti 1956; Isager 1991, 163–167; La Rocca 1998, 228–239 and 2016; F. Coarelli in *LTUR*, I (1993), 133–135.

13 Bravi 2014, 100 (also 2012, 82) understands both *admiratio* and the verb *spectari* as "eine Wahrnehmung der ästhetischen Werte, die eine aufmerksame, konzentrierte und zeitlich nicht eingeschränkte Betrachtung voraussetzt". While this interpretation of Pollio's desired attitude is correct, it does not account for the difference between *admiratio* and the action of *spectari*—the former being a consequence of the latter.

14 On Pollio's career as reflected in his *monumenta*, see Bravi 2012, 82–93; 2014, 95–110. On his biography, see also Canfora 2007, 72–77; Osgood 2006, 251–255.

15 Gualandi 1982, 267 points to Pliny's preference for 'museum-like' displays, which underscore the artworks' relationship to architecture. On the late-Hellenistic taste for delicate artworks that are slightly smaller than life-size, to be viewed frontally, see Zanker 1998, 547–548. Beagon 2011 engages with the topics of sight and gaze in the *Natural History*, while Murphy 2004, 131–133 notes that in the *Natural History* the world is at times presented as "legible to a single surveying eye".

16 *Nat.* 36.21 mentions the shrine at Cnidus for Praxiteles' *Aphrodite*, which was open all around, so as to make the masterpiece visible from all sides. The praise for circular openness aligns with optic preoccupations regarding the possibility that visual magnitude (i.e., viewing an object from more than one angle) could prevent any decrease in image quality owing to distance (see Thibodeau 2016, 140, referring to Euclid's *Optics*, Definition 7, on which see Lindberg 1976, 12).

17 A. Corso in Pliny-Conte 1982–1988, V, 593–594 note 9, 890. *Nat.* 35.157–158 seems to contradict this comment and praises ancient terracottas placed on the roofs of temples. Here, however, Pliny is not referring to any individual context. He is aiming to juxtapose the sober habits of the past and the extravagance of the present.

18 Pliny comments on the anatomy of human eyes in *Nat.* 11.148. There, he refers to the pupil as a narrow "window" which prevents the gaze from wandering around uncertain and "canalises its direction".

19 Vitruvius, *On Architecture* 3.5.9. On the Stoic theory of perception, see Thibodeau 2016, 139; Todd 1974.

20 *Nat.* 35.18. The emperor's transgression is frustrated by material itself (*si tectorii natura permisisset*).

21 The temple, which burnt down in 31 BCE, was restored by Augustus in the following years, see F. Coarelli in *LTUR*, I (1993), 260–261; A. Corso in Pliny-Conte 1982–1988, V, 479.

22 Scholars understand Pliny's words, *ligneis formis inclusum*, as referring to wooden frames (Pliny-Rackham 1961, 389; Pliny-Croisille 1985, 111 and 103; Pliny-Conte 1982–1988, V, 495; Pliny-Ferri 2000, 265; Pliny-König, Winkler 2007, 129). Translations for the passage by Vitruvius are less straightforward (Gwilt 1826, 59: "packed up in wooden cases"; A. Corso in Gros 1997, 145: "forme di legno"; Ferri 2002, 149: "inquadrate poi in telai di legno"), allowing for the possibility that what is meant here is the wooden cases employed for the transport of paintings and mosaic *emblemata*, such as those found at Kenchreai (Ibrahim, Scranton, and Brill 1976, figs. 9–12, Drawing IVB).

23 Nichols 2017, 38–40 comments about this episode that "Greek plunder became Roman knowledge". Squire 2017, 240 describes the practice as 'deframing' and 'reframing'.

24 Salvadori 2016, 478–485, 479–480; Esposito 2017, 266–267; Salvo 2018, 31–32 (who believes that *Nat.* 35.26–27 also refers to this practice).

25 Simmel 1902. Being neither "quite image" nor "a simple object belonging to the surrounding area", the frame becomes, following Stoichita 1997, 30, the threshold between two ontological dimensions.

26 On the concept of 'detached gaze', see Grethlein 2017 (at 168–169, he highlights the temporal dimension of seeing a picture, commenting that "the duration of our attention is also less determined in the case of pictures. We can read slowly or quickly, but the length of a book gives us certain parameters. It is notoriously hard though to decide when we have fully viewed a picture").

27 On the value of *ingenium*, see Rouveret 1989, 342–345; Robert 1995, 301. The role of *ingenium* is a central concern of Book 36, see e.g., *Nat.* 36.81, 96, as well as passages devoted to compositions created *ex uno lapide* or *ex eodem lapide* (*Nat.* 36.34, 36, 37, 41, on which see Settis 1999, 79–81).

28 In *Nat.* 36.2 Pliny criticises the levelling of hills and the construction of ships to transport marble (for negative comments on the practice of digging the earth or foraging the depth of the sea in search of resources cf. *Nat.* 2.158, 12.2, 22.3, 33.1–3 and 73–77; for an example—with moral undertones—of a botched construction of a channel, the Isthmus of Corinth, see *Nat.* 4.10). These activities are praised at later points in the same book, e.g., at *Nat.* 36.104 (on the construction of tunnels for drainage), 36.123 (on the tunnels of aqueducts), and 36.69–70 (on the *difficultas* of moving obelisks from Egypt to Rome). The Roman interest in feats of landscape engineering is a well-known phenomenon, as is made clear by the inscription on Trajan's column in Rome, which details the urban changes, such as flattening the slope at that point, required by

the emperor's forum (*CIL* 6.960 = *ILS* 294). The inscription of the mid-second-century CE surveyor and architect Nonius Datus from Lambaesis (in today's Algeria) demonstrates that expressing this kind of pride was by no means exclusive to the highest echelons of Roman society (*CIL* 7. 2728, 18122 = *ILS* 5795). Pliny, however, adds that what made the obelisk placed by Augustus in the Campus Martius truly marvelous was the ingenuity (*ingenio*) of its new use (*mirabilem usum*) as a *horologium* marking time thanks to its shadow (*Nat.* 36.72).

29 On ancient 'collections', see Rouveret 1987a and 1987b; Chevallier 1991; Bounia 2004; Gahtan and Pegazzano 2015; Shaya 2015. On the 'urban topography' of art in Rome, see also Poggio 2019 and 2020.

30 Apparently contradicting the opinions that he had expressed in the speech, Agrippa kept purchasing art for himself (*Nat.* 35.26). Pliny's veiled criticism seems to include Agrippa's decorative choices in his Baths, where he placed small paintings (*parvas tabellas*) on the walls of the warmest spaces (*in* [...] *calidissima parte*, probably the *laconicum*; the wall decoration in the Baths of Agrippa is discussed again in *Nat.* 36.189). A passage by Vitruvius (*On Architecture* 7.4.4), criticising the choice of decorating winter rooms with "large pictures and delicate ornaments", which would be damaged by the smoke of heating implements, suggests that Agrippa's choice to decorate warm spaces with pictures may be construed as inappropriate. His error of judgement was corrected a short time before Pliny's treatise (*paulo ante*), in the course of restorations (*cum reficerentur*). Pliny's ambivalence towards Agrippa is not surprising given his legacy, for his family lineage would eventually produce Caligula and Nero (*Nat.* 7.45; see Beagon 2005, 197–198). Key to disentangling this question is the meaning of *verum eadem illa torvitas* in *Nat.* 35.26 as referring to Agrippa's behaviour and the possible contrast to his public image (Pliny-Jex-Blake, Sellers 1896: "yet the rude Agrippa"; Pliny-Rackham 1961: "however, that same severe spirit"; Pliny-Croisille 1985: "ce même esprit sourcilleux", see also the commentary on p. 148; R. Mugellesi in Pliny-Conte 1982–1988, V: "ciò nondimeno quel rozzo individuo"; Pliny-Ferri 2000: "ciò non di meno questo rude romano"; Pliny-König, Winkler 2007: "sogar dieser finstere Mann"). The adversarial form suggests that Pliny may be referring to the divergence between public and private behaviours, as hinted by Hrychuk Kontokosta 2019, 58. On the figure of Agrippa in the *Natural History*, see Burns 1964; Roddaz 1984, 512–518.

31 Thorburn 2008 argues that Suetonius presents Tiberius as progressively withdrawn from the Roman body politic. Suetonius highlights Tiberius' lack of interest in the collective good, remarking that he built no magnificent public building during his principate, leaving incomplete the few projects that he undertook (*Tiberius* 47.1). Cassius Dio (*Roman History* 57.10.1–2) and Tacitus (*Annals* 2.49), however, record that Tiberius completed several projects begun by Augustus.

32 On Famulus, see A. Corso in Pliny-Conte 1982–1988, V, 421 note 1, 423–425 note 1; Bradley 2009, 106–108. The 'prison' of Famulus' 'forgotten art' is in striking contrast to the humble shelters where, according to Pliny (*Nat.* 35.84 and 118), Apelles and Protogenes used to work (and live).

33 Suetonius, *Tiberius* 43 uses the term *sellaria* in reference to the rooms in the emperor's villa at Capri, allegedly designed for sexual encounters and the enjoyment of erotic art, see Varner 2017, 254.

34 According to Welch 2007, 158, Pliny's mention of plundered artworks displayed in the *Domus Aurea* may refer to pieces owned by the elite families proscribed after the Pisonian conspiracy in 65 CE.

35 Pliny also criticises the private enjoyment of art in *Nat.* 36.6, 48, 110–111, 115, 117 (see also *Nat.* 31.42 on the redirection towards private countryside villas of the water from the aqueducts, which were meant to serve the city of Rome). A paradigm example of private misuse of art is the house of Scaurus, which Pliny presents in strikingly similar terms to Nero's *Domus Aurea* (*Nat.* 36.117). Criticism of private appropriation of art is by no means limited to Pliny's *Natural History* and has been widely used by other Latin authors to reinforce the negative construction of individuals—as is famously the case with Cicero's portrayal of Verres, the corrupt governor of Sicily (see Miles 2002 and 2008; Weis 2003).

36 Literary sources present Nero's *Domus Aurea* as an oversized villa (Suetonius, *Nero* 31), where one could enjoy solitude and open landscapes (Tacitus, *Annals* 15.42). On Nero's transgression of boundaries between *rus* and *urbs*, see Elsner 1994. Tacitus emphasises the architects' *ingenium* and *audacia* in overturning the rules of Nature. Both Suetonius and Tacitus highlight the taste for sliding walls and veneering. On Suetonius' account of the *Domus Aurea*, see Bradley 1978, 171–181. That period's taste for deceptive ceilings is apparent in public architecture too; see Suetonius, *Nero* 31 and *ibidem* 34, where the technology of ceilings with sliding panels is mentioned again in a much darker context, Nero's attempts at murdering his own mother. In *Nat.* 19.24, Pliny mentions the practice in the age of Nero of covering the space of amphitheatres with tents (*vela*) of the color of the sky and spangled with stars. Again, we are confronted with an absurd search for illusion—created by a tent which imitates the (invisible) sky above.

37 Cf. *Nat.* 33.54. Only a few years later, Martial resorted to the same imagery in articulating the conflict between *urbs* and *domus* over the *Domus Aurea* (*Spectacles* 2.4). The presentation of Nero's *Domus Aurea* as a suffocating enclosure is reminiscent of Pliny's praise of the ancient borders of Rome (*Nat.* 3.67), which provided the safety required for growth and expansion.

38 Isager 1991, 224–229 and 2006a explores Pliny's construction of Nero and Vespasian as opposing ethical paradigms. On the Flavian emperors' engagement with the artistic and monumental landscape of Rome, see Baldwin 1995, 59–60; Darwall-Smith 1996, 35–40; Packer 2003; Gallia 2016; Varner 2017.

39 The 'periegetic presentation' of marble sculpture starts at *Nat.* 36.13, where the presence of marble statues in Rome is linked to this art's beginnings. Isager 1991, 159–168 discusses the sections of Book 36 dedicated to the public collections of sculpture in Rome.

40 Scholars have often remarked that the *Natural History* is a 'literary counterpart' of Rome; see, e.g., Carey 2000 and 2003, 75–101; Naas 2002, 449–472; Isager 2006b, 125.

41 *Judaic War* 7.159–160; see Naas 2002, 460–468; Chapman 2009, 111–117. On the art collection in the *Templum Pacis*, see La Rocca 2001, 196–200; Isager 2006a; Tucci 2007, 216–258; Bravi 2012, 167–181 and 2014, 203–226. On the ideological dimension of the complex, see Naas 2002, 438–446; Noreña 2003.

42 For discussion, see Tucci 2017, 60–61; Macaulay-Lewis 2011, 280–283. Re-
    cent accounts of elongated structures as garden plots are in Gallia 2016,
    153; Pollard 2009; see also Lloyd 1982, 91–93. La Rocca 2001, 195–207 sup-
    ports identification as water basins.
43 Pollard 2009, drawing on the concept of 'ecological imperialism' employed
    by Crosby 1986.
44 See Tucci 2017, 60–61 on the irrigation system in the *Templum Pacis*.
45 Macaulay-Lewis 2011, 283–284. On the importance of parallel strolling
    paths and eye-level displays in the design of Roman gardens, see Gleason
    2020; Gleason, Palmer, Allen, and Bai 2020.
46 The idea of 'alternative worlds' first surfaces in *Nat.* 2.3 and becomes clear
    in Book 9 about marine animals, where Pliny stresses the concept that
    underwater lifeforms mirror those on earth (*Nat.* 9.2). See A. Borghini in
    Pliny-Conte 1982–1988, II (1983), 293–294. Pliny also describes the island
    of Sri Lanka (*Taprobane*) as "another world" (*Nat.* 6.81) and a place "out-
    side the world" (*Nat.* 6.89), unknown to the Romans until recent times (see
    Vial-Logeay 2010). For the scientific and literary context of Pliny's pre-
    sentation of places at the 'extreme' frontiers of the world, see Romm 1992.

Conclusion

Pliny's stance on the importance of artistic processes is clearest in his presentation of the two first-century BCE artists, Pasiteles and Arcesilaus, discussed in the Introduction to this volume. Both are praised for their ability to work with different materials and for investing significant effort in the visual manifestation of their thought process.[1] Pliny stresses the functional and intellectual link between a work of art and its preliminary models also in discussing artists from the age of Alexander the Great when, according to his evolutionary paradigm, Greek art reached its pinnacle. Pliny believes that Lysistratus of Sicyon, the brother of Lysippus, should be credited with discovering the technique of "taking casts from statues" (*Nat.* 35.153: *de signis effigies exprimere invenit*). This invention was reportedly so successful that afterwards "no figures or statues were made without a clay model".[2] The role of preliminary models is essential to the section on Apelles (*Nat.* 35.92, 145). Fascination with his unfinished *Aphrodite* at Cos emanates from the work's twofold nature as a real object (the unfinished painting) and an intellectual object (Apelles' idea). The artist's groundwork becomes synonymous with his thought process.

Parallels between the careers of Apelles and Arcesilaus go beyond their shared proficiency in preparatory models. Like Apelles, Arcesilaus also seems to owe his fame to a fascination with incompletion, as both of his major projects—the statue of *Venus Genetrix* for display in Caesar's Forum and the statue of *Felicitas* for Lucius Lucullus—indeed remained unfinished (*Nat.* 35.156). Work on the *Felicitas* stopped following the death of both Arcesilaus and Lucullus. The statue of *Venus* was left incomplete in the haste to dedicate it within the new forum. In this anecdote, finitude depends on a negotiation between the artist and his patron. The image of Venus clearly looked finished enough to Cesar and, one might infer, to the visitors of his forum.

As this book has demonstrated, the discussion of artistic materials and processes illustrates important points about history, social practices, and philosophical or ideological views. In mentioning the origin of clay models for sculpture, which were allegedly invented by Lysistratus and fully exploited by Pasiteles and Arcesilaus, Pliny adds a cursory yet crucial comment: he states that the technique of modelling in clay (*hanc scientiam*) was "older than that of casting bronze" (*Nat.* 35.153). A few paragraphs later, he remarks "that art" (*hanc artem*) had already been brought to perfection in Italy (*Nat.* 35.157). It thus becomes clear that the point in question is less a 'neutral' sequence of events and more the construction of a history of technological progress wherein Rome holds a place comparable to Greece. This preoccupation emerges at other points of the treatise as the narrative suggests the traditional Roman origins for the principal techniques.[3]

Pliny approaches Rome's historical past as an instrument to account for the present. His interest in the relationship between the Roman past and present is rooted in a perception of his contemporaries' progressive estrangement from traditional wisdom and values. Pliny's exploration of oblivion as a product of time (and thus Nature) takes on a more elaborate shape in the final books of the treatise. There, he discusses instances of *obliteratio* due to a lack of time for leisurely consideration and the fate of oblivion that befell Nero's images, buildings, and trusted artists. He castigates ostentation in the private sphere as a futile endeavour, noting that even the finest house in Rome appears insignificant and largely forgotten only a generation after it was built (*Nat.* 36.109). On the contrary, halls decorated with the dignified portraits of previous owners made in humble wax ensure that the past remains forever 'present' (*Nat.* 35.7). Materials participate in this discourse about time. As a substance appreciated exclusively for its monetary value, gold prevents the recognition of human skill and thus the memory of artists' names (*Nat.* 33.154). Other materials are also discussed in light of their process of decay or maintenance.[4] Pliny's fascination with the signs of age, especially in the case of metal surfaces, reflects the widespread taste of his time. The greenish hue of statues made of exotic basanite, produced in considerable number since the early imperial period, emulated the calligraphic quality of metalwork and the dark patina of old bronze (Figure C.1).[5] The production of lead-glazed pottery taps into the same attraction to objects that cross material boundaries and defy expectations by imitating not only different substances, but also different states of preservation (Figure C.2).

At the roots of Pliny's castigation of *luxuria* lies the idea of a moral shift from past austerity to a decadent present. This idea is commonplace in Roman literature, along with the connection between decline and imperial expansion.[6] The contradictions within this concept are inescapable. In *Nat.* 13.23, Pliny acknowledges the ambiguities of the Roman appetite for exotic goods as he depicts "the eagles and the

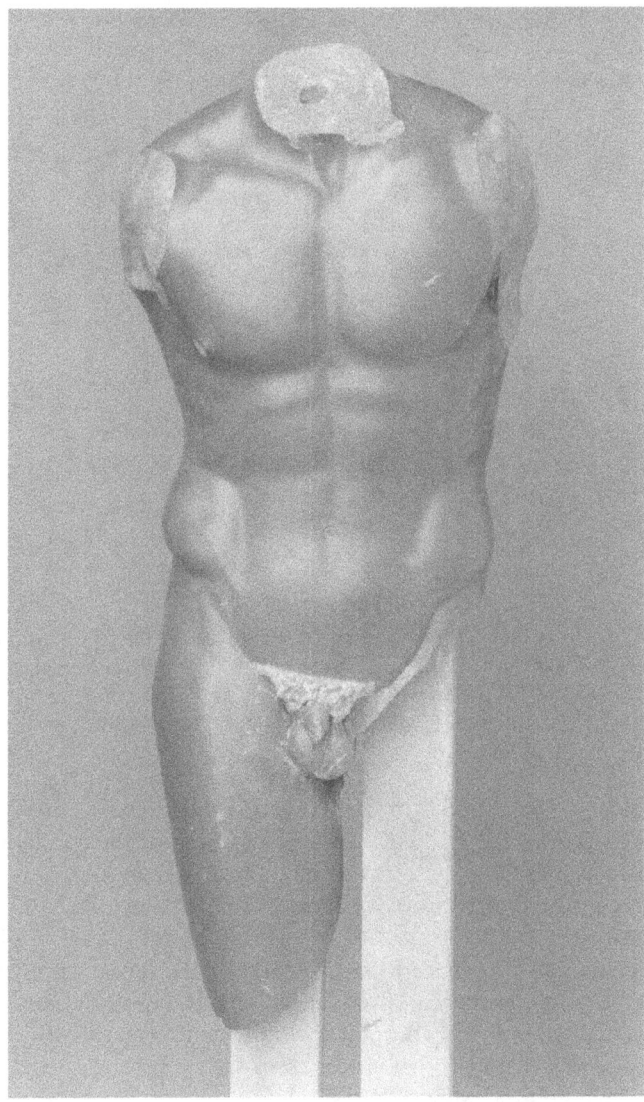

Figure C.1 Statue of an athlete, first century CE. Basanite. H 110 cm. Castel Gandolfo, Musei Vaticani, Villa Pontificia, Antiquarium, inv. no. 36405.

Credit: Rome, German Archaeological Institute (D-DAI-ROM-66.2400, G. Singer).

standards" in Roman camps being "anointed" with lavish Eastern perfumes—and yet capable of conquering the world. Within the *Natural History*, the place of monetary worth is equally ambivalent. Pliny

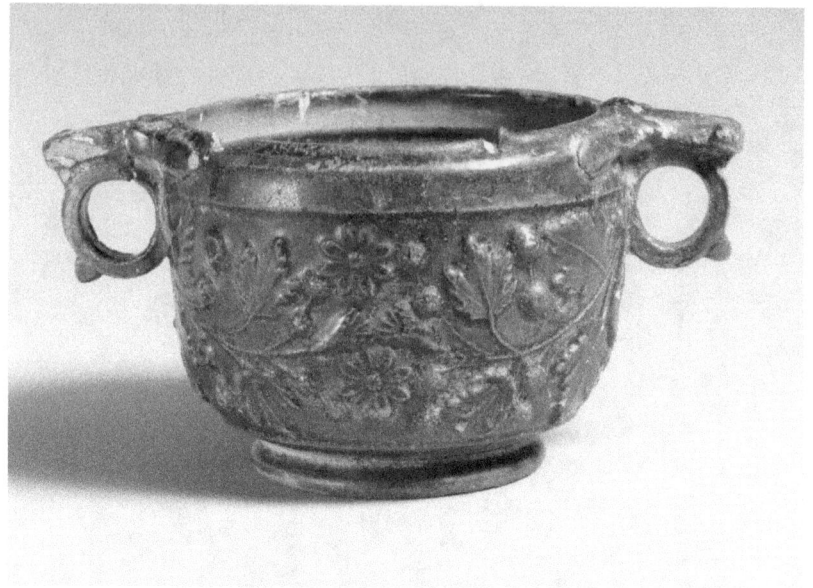

Figure C.2 Cup (*skyphos*), first half of the first century CE. Terracotta, lead-glazed ware. H 7.8 cm. New York, Metropolitan Museum of Art, inv. no. 29.100.77.

Credit: New York, Metropolitan Museum of Art, Open Content Programme.

relies heavily on instances of extravagant pricing to organise a hierarchy of artworks and his work closes with a list of the most valuable materials (*Nat.* 37.204).[7] However, he cannot fail to find evaluations based on commercial desirability at odds with his morality.[8] Returning to the case used to open this book, anecdotes about the skill of Pasiteles and Arcesilaus outshine Pliny's (reluctant) presentation of materials according to commercial preoccupations. It is no coincidence that Pasiteles himself is listed among the notable engravers of silver; Pliny observes how, given its inferior monetary value, silver allowed craftsmen to reach greater esteem than gold.

One novelty in Pliny's approach is his articulation of tight semantics for artistic materials and techniques to elucidate broader points about social expectations, tradition, and ethics. The encyclopaedia is exceptional in its pragmatic effort to address perceived moral and intellectual weaknesses by means of a straightforwardly practical instrument. Expansion, according to Pliny's argument, is about *growth* as well as *oblivion*: "Owing to their greatness (*magnitudo*), the Roman people have lost their usages (*perdidit ritus*)" (*Nat.* 24.5)[9]. Citing the expansion (*maiestas*) of Rome and the consequent improvement in trade and communication, Pliny observes that things "that had previously lain concealed" were now in general use (*Nat.* 14.2–3). In this perspective, the challenge (*labor*) of the encyclopaedia lies in both investigating new discoveries (*postea inventa*) and preserving traditional wisdom (*ea quae invenerant prisci*). Pliny's catalogue complements the experience of first-century CE Romans encountering and claiming new resources, and then integrating them into their cultural framework and everyday life. At the same time, the encyclopaedia provides a repository of 'conventional' wisdom, to ensure continued relevance of Roman traditions. Pliny reclaims the memory of what has been neglected over time, constructs the 'correct' memory of new facts, and exploits the potential for memory to obscure persons and things with negative ethical connotations. The encyclopaedia's new, selective memory presents readers who are able to "devote themselves leisurely to their studies" (*Praef.* 6) with a permanent, self-contained, easily accessed repository of knowledge. It also offers a reflection on how memory is formed, preserved, and transmitted, along with the social implications of these mechanisms.[10]

Pliny is keenly aware of the link between his purpose of 'crystallising' memory and the problem of selection (*Nat.* 35.1).[11] For an encyclopedia, careful consideration of authorial responsibility and self-determination in the selection of subjects, facts, and information is obviously a central concern. In this sense, Pliny's discussion of ingenuity, integrity, diligence, invention, finitude, and perception in the artistic realm—all concepts developed in the six chapters of this book—reflects his preoccupation with the peculiar challenges of his kind of 'production'.[12] Pliny exploits the visual potential of artistic materials and processes not only to construct a corpus of moral *exempla*, but also as an explicit metaphor for his own choices and challenges as a writer. For these reasons, discourse on the substances and processes of art provides an exceptional standpoint for investigation. This investigation explores how the *Natural History* presents itself as part of a monumental landscape that is both material and immaterial, composed of public buildings that serve the city of Rome and the literary *labores* with the mission of preserving and enhancing Rome's collective memory.

Notes

1 Pliny discusses the use of models in the case of Nero's Colossus (*Nat.* 34.46). The role of this artwork in constructing the image of Nero's 'artistic

transgression' and Vespasian's restoration of traditional values explains the extraordinary space that Pliny gives to the first-hand account of his visit to Zenodorus' workshop. See also the story about the preliminary drawings (*graphidis vestigia*) made by the Classical painter Parrhasius, allegedly used as models by other artists (*Nat.* 35.68).

2 Pliny-Rackham 1961, 375. See also Pliny-Conte 1982–1988, V, 477; Pliny-König, Winkler 2007, 117; Pliny-Jex-Blake, Sellers 1968, 177; Pliny-Croisille 1985, 102, 263–264. The best account is Henke 2020.

3 See also *Nat.* 34.15, 33–34; and 35.17–19, 35.22, 35.115–116. On Pliny's construction of a Roman artistic past, see Croisille 1987; De Angelis 2008; Smith 2007. Naas 2002, 101–103 and 2011b engage with the issue of philhellenism and Roman identity in the *Natural History*.

4 E.g., in *Nat.* 34.99 and 140–141, 143, 146; 37.70–71, 109, 134.

5 See J. Daehner in Daehner and Lapatin 2015, 280–281 no. 44.

6 E.g., Livy, *History of Rome* 1.*pr*.12; Sallust, *The War with Catiline* 11–13.

7 On the relationship between *auctoritas* and price in the *Natural History*, see Papini 2020 and Adornato 2020, 97–102. Lao 2011 explores Pliny's attitude to *luxuria* in light of the economic landscape of his time.

8 This is clear in *Nat.* 34.5, where the increase of economic value (*pretium*) is presented as responsible for the degradation of authority (*auctoritas artis*).

9 See Citroni Marchetti 1991, 225; Murphy 2004, 68–71. See also Naas 2002, 402–405.

10 Carey 2003, 138–156 explores Pliny's interest in the mechanism that regulate the perpetuation of memory, with particular reference to portraiture. Literature on 'collective' and 'cultural memory' is extensive: an introduction can be found in Olick, Vinitzky-Seroussi, and Levy 2011, as well as in Erll and Nünning 2008. For a literary exploration of Rome's imagery as a "city of memories", "city of empire", and "city of marvels", see Edwards 1996.

11 See also *Nat.* 34.37 and 53; 35.53; 37.195.

12 For the rhetoric of "writing as production" as a key element in Pliny's concept, see Sinclair 2003.

Bibliography

Acosta-Hughes, B., Kosmetatou, E., and Baumbach, M. (eds.) 2004. *Labored in Papyrus Leaves*. Washington. <http://nrs.harvard.edu/urn-3:hul.ebook:CHS_AcostaHughesB_etal_eds.Labored_in_Papyrus_Leaves.2004> (last accessed 6th September 2020).

Adornato, G. 2007. "Sguardi letterari e giudizi d'arte: Lisippo e gli artisti dell'ἀλήθεια", in De Angelis 2007, 3–18.

———. 2015. *"Aletheia/Veritas*: The New Canon", in Daehner and Lapatin 2015, 49–59.

———. 2019a. "Kritios and Nesiotes as Revolutionary Artists? Ancient and Archaeological Perspectives on the So-Called Severe Style Period", *AJA* 123, no. 4: 557–587.

———. 2019b. *"Pondus, uno crure*, and Polykleitos' Statues", in H.R. Goette and I. Leventi (eds.), *Excellence. Studies in Honour of Olga Palagia*. Rahden, 45–59.

———. 2019c. "The Invention of the Classical Style in Sculpture", in O. Palagia (ed.), *Handbook of Greek Sculpture*. Berlin and Boston, 311–326.

———. 2020. *"Ut etiam fictilia pluris constent quam murrina*. Art Market, Canons, and Archaeological Evidence", in Adornato, Cirucci, and Cupperi 2020, 95–112.

Adornato, G., Cirucci, G., and Cupperi, W. (eds.) 2020. *Beyond "Art Collections". Owning and Accumulating Objects from Greek Antiquity to the Early Modern Period*. Berlin and Boston.

Adornato, G., Falaschi, E., and Poggio, A. (eds.) 2019. Περὶ γραφικῆς. *Pittori, tecniche, trattati, contesti tra testimonianze e ricezione*. Milano.

Adornato, G., Romano, L.B., Cirucci, G., and Poggio, A. (eds.) 2018. *Restaging Greek Artworks in Roman Times*. Milano.

Albertson, F.C. 2001. "Zenodorus' Colossus of Nero", *MAAR* 46: 95–118.

Allen, R. 2019. "Eye-Like Radiance: The Depiction of Gemstones in Roman Wall Painting", *Arts* 8, no. 2: 60. <https://doi.org/10.3390/arts8020060> (last accessed 6th September 2020).

André, J.-M. 1966. *L'otium dans la vie morale et intellectuelle romaine*. Paris.

Anguissola, A. 2005. "Roman Copies of Myron's *Discobolus*", *JRA* 18: 317–335.

———. 2006. "Parole e contesto nel discorso pliniano sull'imitazione artistica", *RAL* s. 9, 17: 555–572.

———. 2007a. "Fama, tema, forma: fortuna antica e moderna del *Discobolo* di Mirone", *Prospettiva* 128: 26–42.

———. 2007b. "Persone e oggetti nel *cubiculum*: la costruzione letteraria della privacy nella casa romana", in De Angelis 2007, 149–167.

———. 2010. *Intimità a Pompei. Riservatezza, condivisione e prestigio negli ambienti ad alcova di Pompei.* Berlin and New York.

———. 2012. *'Difficillima imitatio'. Immagine e lessico delle copie tra Grecia e Roma.* Roma.

———. 2018. *Supports in Roman Marble Sculpture. Workshop Practice and Modes of Viewing.* Cambridge.

———. 2020. "The Materiality of Creation. Integrity, Deception, and the Process of Art", in Anguissola and Grüner 2020, 132–144.

———. Forthcoming. "Ethical Matters. Pliny the Elder on Material Deception", in A. Haug and A. Hielscher (eds.), *Materiality as Decor.* Berlin and Boston.

Anguissola, A., and Faedo, L. Forthcoming. "Lo sguardo di Plinio tra tecnica e materia: le statue e la loro superficie", in M. Collareta, M. Ferretti, S. Maffei, and C.M. Sicca (eds.), *Le parole del marmo.*

Anguissola, A., and Grüner, A. (eds.) 2020. *The Nature of Art. Pliny the Elder on Materials.* Turnhout.

Arnaud, P. 2007. "Introduction: La géographie romaine impériale, entre tradition et innovation", in G. Cruz Andreotti, P. Le Roux, and P. Moret (eds.), *La invención de una geografía de la Península Ibérica. II. La época imperial.* Málaga and Madrid, 13–46.

Artmann, B. 1993. "Roman Dodecahedra", *The Mathematical Intelligencer* 15, no. 2: 52–53.

———. 1996. "A Roman Icosahedron Discovered", *The American Mathematical Monthly* 103, no. 2: 132–133.

Ash, R. 2011. "Pliny the Elder's Attitude to Warfare", in Gibson and Morello 2011, 1–19.

Austin, R.G. 1944. "Quintilian on Painting and Statuary", *CQ* 38: 17–26.

Baar, M. 1990. *Das Bild des Kaisers Tiberius bei Tacitus, Sueton und Cassius Dio.* Stuttgart.

Bäbler, B. 2002. "Auf der Suche nach Xenokrates: gab es Kunstgeschichte in der Antike?", *SemRom* 5, 137–160.

Badel, C. 2006. "Pline l'Ancien et la 'mémoire perdue' de l'invention technique à Rome", in M.-S. Corcy, C. Douyère-Demeulenaere, and L. Hilaire-Pérez (eds.), *Les archives de l'invention.* Toulouse. <doi: https://doi.org/10.4000/books.pumi.40828> (last accessed 23 December 2020).

Baldwin, B. 1995. "Roman Emperors in the Elder Pliny", *Scholia* n.s., 4: 56–78.

Ballestrazzi, C. 2020. "Arte senza storia? I *nobiles artifices* delle gemme e il loro destino", *RA* 70: 359–385.

Barrett, J. 2009. *Vibrant Matter: A Political Ecology of Things.* Durham and London.

Barton, T. 1994. "The *Inventio* of Nero: Suetonius", in Elsner and Masters 1994, 48–63.

Bartsch, S., Freudenburg, K., and Littlewood, C. (eds.) 2017. *The Cambridge Companion to the Age of Nero*. Cambridge, 195–212.

Beagon, M. 1992. *Roman Nature. The Thought of Pliny the Elder*. Oxford.

———. 1996. "Nature and Her Landscapes in Pliny the Elder", in G. Shipley and J. Salmon (eds.), *Human Landscapes in Classical Antiquity: Environment and Culture*. London, 284–329.

———. 2001. "Plinio, la tradizione enciclopedica e i *mirabilia*", in *Storia della scienza*, I. Roma, 735–745.

———. 2005. *The Elder Pliny on the Human Animal. Natural History Book 7*. Oxford.

———. 2007. "Situating Nature's Wonders in Pliny's *Natural History*", in Bispham and Rowe 2007, 19–40.

———. 2011. "The Curious Eye of the Elder Pliny", in Gibson and Morello 2011, 71–88.

———. 2013. "*Labores pro Bono Publico*: the Burdensome Mission of Pliny's *Natural History*", in König and Woolf 2013a, 84–107.

Beard, M. 2007. *The Roman Triumph*. Cambridge, MA and London.

Becatti, G. 1951. *Arte e gusto negli scrittori latini*. Firenze.

———. 1956. "Letture pliniane: le opere d'arte nei *Monumenta Asini Pollionis* e negli *Horti Serviliani*", in E. Arslan (ed.), *Studi in onore di Aristide Calderini e Roberto Paribeni*, III. Milan and Varese, 199–210.

Belloni, L. 2016. "Una rarità imperfetta (*P. Mil. Vogl.* VIII 309, III 8–13 = 16 A. – B. = 16 S. – St. – W.)", *ExClass* 20: 7–18.

Bergmann, M. 1994. *Der Koloß Neros, die Domus Aurea und der Mentalitätswandel im Rom der frühen Kaiserzeit*. Mainz am Rhein.

———. 2013. "Portraits of an Emperor. Nero, the Sun, and Roman *Otium*", in Buckley and Dinter 2013, 332–362.

Berry, C.J. 1994. *The Idea of Luxury. A Conceptual and Historical Investigation*. Cambridge.

Bispham, E. 2007. "Pliny the Elder's Italy", in Bispham and Rowe 2007, 41–67.

Bispham, E., and Rowe, G., (eds., with E. Matthews). 2007. *'Vita vigilia est'. BICS. Supplement* 100.

Blonski, M. 2007. "Pline, les Perses, le parfum: analyse d'un fantasme", *RPh* 81, no. 1: 13–24.

Bodson, L. 1986. "La zoologie romaine d'après la *NH* de Pline", *Helmantica* 37: 107–116.

Bounia, A. 2004. *The Nature of Classical Collecting*. Aldershot.

Boyle, A., and Dominik, W.J. (eds.) 2003. *Flavian Rome: Culture, Image, Text*. Leiden and Boston.

Bradley, K.R. 1978. *Suetonius' Life of Nero. An Historical Commentary*. Bruxelles.

Bradley, M. 2009. *Colour and Meaning in Ancient Rome*. Cambridge.

———. 2013. "Colour as Synaesthetic Experience in Antiquity", in S. Butler and A. Purves (eds.), *Synaesthesia and the Ancient Senses*. Durham, 127–140.

Bravi, A. 2012. *'Ornamenta Urbis'. Opere d'arte greche negli spazi romani.* Bari.
———. 2014. *Griechische Kunstwerke im politischen Leben Roms und Konstantinopels.* Berlin.
Brodersen, K. 2003. *Terra Cognita. Studien zur römischen Raumerfassung.* Zürich and New York.
Buckley, E., and Dinter, M.T. (eds.) 2013. *A Companion to the Neronian Age.* Chichester.
Buettner, B. 2020. "Icy Geometry: Rock Crystal in Lapidary Knowledge", in Hahn and Shalem 2020, 117–128.
Burns, M.A.T. 1964. "Pliny's Ideal Roman", *CJ* 59, no. 6: 253–258.
Butini, E. 2019. *Enigma Dei Vasi Murrini.* Rome.
Cadario, M. 2014. "Preparing for Triumph. *Graecae Artes* as Roman Booty in L. Mummius' Campaign (146 BC)", in C.H. Lange and F.K. Vervaet (eds.), *The Roman Republican Triumph Beyond the Spectacle.* Roma, 83–101.
Caley, E.R., and Richards, J.F.C. 1956. *Theophrastus. On Stones,* with introduction, Greek text, transl., and commentary by E.R. Caley and J.F.C. Richrds. Columbus.
Canfora, L. 2007. *Julius Caesar. The People's Dictator.* Edinburgh.
Carey, S. 2000. "The Problem of Totality. Collecting Greek Art, Wonders, and Luxury in Pliny the Elder's *Natural History*", *Journal of the History of Collections* 12, no. 1: 1–13.
———. 2003. *Pliny's Catalogue of Culture: Art and Empire in the Natural History.* Oxford.
Casson, L. 1978. "Unemployment, the Building Trade, and Suetonius, *Vesp.* 18", *BASP* 15, no. 1–2: 43–51.
Catoni, M.L. 2020. "Parian Marble and *quella che si fa per forza di levare*", in Anguissola and Grüner 2020, 157–170.
Cecconi, G.A. 2007. "*Res, historiae, observationes* a tema militare e la legittimazione dei principi: passato e presente in Plinio il Vecchio", in P. Desideri, S. Roda, and A.M. Biraschi, in cooperation with A. Pellizzari (eds.), *Costruzione e uso del passato storico nella cultura antica.* Alessandria, 313–337.
Celkyte, A. 2017. "The Stoic Definition of Beauty as *Summetria*", *CQ* 67: 88–425.
Champlin, E. 2008. "Tiberius the Wise", *Historia* 57, no. 4: 408–425.
Chapman, H.H. 2009. "What Josephus Sees: The Temple of Peace and the Jerusalem Temple as Spectacle in Text and Art", *Phoenix* 63, no. 1–2: 107–130.
Chevallier, R. 1986. "Le bois, l'arbre et la forêt chez Pline", *Helmantica* 37: 147–172.
———. 1991. *L'artiste, le collectionneur et le faussaire.* Paris.
Citroni Marchetti, S. 1982. "*Iuvare mortalem.* L'ideale programmatico della *Naturalis Historia* di Plinio nei rapporti con il moralismo stoico-diatribico", *A&R* 27, no. 3–4: 124–148.
———. 1991. *Plinio il Vecchio e la tradizione del moralismo romano.* Pisa.

————. 1992. "Filosofia e ideologia nella *Naturalis Historia* di Plinio", in *ANRW*, II, 36.5, 3249–3306.

————. 2005a. "Le scelte di un intellettuale: sulle motivazioni culturali della *Naturalis Historia*", *MD* 54: 91–121.

————. 2005b. *"Quid ista legis…?* La prefazione alla *Naturalis Historia* e il programma di (non) scrivere per il principe e il contadino", in F. Gasti and G. Mazzoli (eds.), *Modelli letterari e ideologia nell'età flavia*. Pavia, 39–56.

————. 2011. *La scienza della natura per un intellettuale romano*. Pisa and Roma.

————. 2017. *"Contingat aliqua gratia operae curaeque nostrae*: An Ethic of Care in the *Naturalis Historia*", in F. Bessone and M. Fucecchi (eds.), *The Literary Genres in the Flavian Age*. Berlin and Boston, 65–82.

————. 2019. "La storia dell'arte nel sistema espressivo e simbolico della *Naturalis Historia*", in Adornato, Falaschi, and Poggio 2019, 233–248.

Conte, G.B. 1982. "L'inventario del mondo. Ordine e linguaggio della natura nell'opera di Plinio il Vecchio", in Pliny-Conte 1982–1988, I (1982), xvii–xlvii.

————. 2012. "L'inventario del mondo. Forma della natura e progetto enciclopedico nell'opera di Plinio il Vecchio", in G.B. Conte, *Generi e lettori*. Pisa (3rd edition): 77–112.

Cook, E.M. 2020. "Pliny the Elder in the Workshop of Zenodorus and the Materiality of Facture in the *Natural History*", in Anguissola and Grüner 2020, 112–125.

Cotta Ramosino, L. 2004. *Plinio il Vecchio e la tradizione storica di Roma nella Naturalis Historia*. Alessandria.

Cotton, H.M., and Eck, W. 1997. "Ein Staatsmonopol und seine Folgen: Plinius, *Naturalis Historia* 12, 123 und der Preis für Balsam", *RhM* n.s., 140, no. 2: 153–161.

Coulson, W.D.E. 1976. "The Reliability of Pliny's Chapters on Greek and Roman Sculpture", *CW* 69, no. 6: 361–372.

Croisille, J.-M. 1987. "Pline et la peinture d'époque romaine", *Helmantica* 38: 5–21.

Crosby, A.W. 1986. *Ecological Imperialism*. Cambridge.

Crowley, P.R. 2016. "Crystalline Aesthetics and the Classical Concept of the Medium", *West 86th* 23, no. 2, 220–251.

————. 2020. "Rock Crystal and the Nature of Artifice in Ancient Rome", in Hahn and Shalem 2020, 151–162.

Daehner, J., and Lapatin, K. (eds.) 2015. *Power and Pathos. Bronze Sculpture of the Hellenistic World*. Los Angeles.

Daneu Lattanzi, A. 1982. "A proposito dei libri sulle arti", in *Plinio il Vecchio sotto il profilo storico e letterario*. Como, 97–107.

Darab, Á. 2012. "Ialysus: The Lack of Description", *ACD* 48: 75–89.

————. 2014a. *"Natura, Ars, Historia*. Anecdotic History of Art in Pliny the Elder's *Naturalis Historia*. Part I", *Hermes* 142, no. 2: 206–224.

————. 2014b. "*Natura, Ars, Historia*. Anecdotic History of Art in Pliny the Elder's *Naturalis Historia*. Part II", *Hermes* 142, no. 3: 279–297.

————. 2015. "*Corinthium aes*. Die Entstehung und Metamorphose einer Anekdote", *WS* 128: 69–82.

Darwall-Smith, R.H. 1996. *Emperors and Architecture: A Study of Flavian Rome*. Bruxelles.

De Angelis, F. (ed.) 2007. *Lo sguardo archeologico. I normalisti per Paul Zanker*. Pisa.

————. 2008. "Pliny the Elder and the Identity of Roman Art", *RES* 53–54: 79–92.

————. 2015. "Greek and Roman Specialized Writing on Art and Architecture", in Marconi 2015, 70–83.

Dekoulakou-Sideris, I. 1990. "A Metrological Relief from Salamis", *AJA* 94, no. 3: 445–451.

Della Corte, F. 1982. "Tecnica espositiva e struttura della *Naturalis Historia*", in *Plinio il Vecchio sotto il profilo storico e letterario*. Como, 19–39.

Demandt, A. 2009. *Alexander der Grosse*. München.

Dilke, O.A.W. 1987. "Maps in the Service of the State: Roman Cartography to the End of the Augustan Era", in J.B. Harley and D. Woodward (eds.), *The History of Cartography*, I. Chicago and London, 201–211.

Doody, A. 2001. "Finding Facts in Pliny's Encyclopaedia: The *Summarium* of the *Natural History*", *Ramus* 30, no. 1: 1–22.

————. 2009. "Pliny's *Natural History: Enkuklios Paideia* and the Ancient Encyclopedia", *JHI* 70, no. 1: 1–21.

————. 2010. *Pliny's Encyclopedia. The Reception of the Natural History*. Cambridge.

————. 2013. "Literature of the World: Seneca's *Natural Questions* and Pliny's *Natural History*", in Buckley and Dinter 2013, 288–301.

Dorandi, T. 2019. "Antigono di Caristo artista e scrittore d'arte", in Adornato, Falaschi, and Poggio 2019, 135–150.

Duarte, P. 2009. "Qu'est-ce que la perfection d'une œuvre d'art pour Pline l'Ancien", *Loxias* 26. <http://revel.unice.fr/loxias/index.html?id=3048> (last accessed 10th September 2020).

Dubois-Pelerin, É. 2008. *Le luxe privé à Rome et en Italie au Ier siècle après J.-C.* Napoli.

Dumont, J.P. 1986. "L'idée du dieu chez Pline", *Helmantica* 37, 219–237.

Edwards, C. 1996. *Writing Rome. Textual Approaches to the City*. Cambridge.

————. 2003. "Incorporating the Alien: The Art of Conquest", in C. Edwards and G. Woolf (eds.), *Rome the Cosmopolis*. Cambridge.

Elsner, J. 1994. "Constructing Decadence: The Representation of Nero as Imperial Builder", in Elsner and Masters 1994, 112–127.

————. 2014. "Lithic Poetics: Posidippus and His Stones", *Ramus* 43, no. 2: 152–172.

Elsner, J., and Masters, J. (eds.) 1994. *Reflections of Nero: Culture, History and Representation*. London.

Ensoli, S. 2002. "Una nuova ipotesi sul Colosso di Nerone. A proposito dei tre frammenti bronzei dei Musei Capitolini", in J.-M. Croisille and Y. Perrin (eds.), *Neronia VI*. Bruxelles, 97–122.

———. 2007. "Il Colosso di Nerone-Sol a Roma: una 'falsa' imitazione del Colosso di Helios a Rodi", in Y. Perrin (ed.), *Neronia VII*. Bruxelles, 406–427.

Erll, A., and Nünning, A. (eds., in collaboration with S.B. Young) 2008. *Cultural Memory Studies*. Berlin and New York.

Erskine, A. 2001. *Troy between Greece and Rome: Local Tradition and Imperial Rome*. Oxford and New York.

Esposito, D. 2016. "Il lavoro degli anonimi. Lo *status quaestionis* delle ricerche sull'operato dei pittori romani", *BABesch* 91: 173–195.

———. 2017. "The Economics of Pompeian Painting", in M. Flohr and A. Wilson (eds.), *The Economy of Pompeii*. Oxford, 263–289.

Faedo, L. 2020. "Gilding: Art and Technique, Vision and Morals", in Anguissola and Grüner 2020, 224–235.

Falaschi, E. 2018. "More than Words. Restaging Protogenes' *Ialysus*. The Many Lives of an Artwork between Greece and Rome", in Adornato, Romano, Cirucci, and Poggio 2018, 173–190.

Fane Saunders, P. 2016. *Pliny the Elder and the Emergence of Renaissance Architecture*. Cambridge.

Favro, D. 1996. *The Urban Image of Augustan Rome*. Cambridge.

Fear, A. 2011. "The Roman's Burden", in Gibson and Morello 2011, 21–34.

Ferraro, V. 1975. "Il numero delle fonti, dei volumi e dei fatti della Naturalis *Historia* di Plinio", *ASNP* s. III, 5: 519–533.

Ferri, S. 1940. "Nuovi contributi esegetici al Cànone della scultura greca", *RIA* 6: 117–142 (= *Opuscula. SCO* 11, 1962: 122–158).

———. 1942a. "Note esegetiche ai giudizi d'arte di Plinio il Vecchio", *ASNP* s. II, 11: 69–116.

———. 1942b. "Tendenza unitaria delle arti nella Grecia antica", *AAPal* 2: 531–560.

———. 1960. "*Diligentia*", in *EAA*, III, 98–99.

———. 1965. "*Quadratus*", in *EAA*, VI, 586–587.

———. 2002: *Vitruvio Pollione, Architettura (dai libri I-VII)*, ed. and transl. by S. Ferri. Milano.

Flemming, R. 2005. "Empires of Knowledge: Medicine and Health in the Hellenistic World", in A. Erskine (ed.), *A Companion to the Hellenistic World*. Malden, MA and Oxford, 449–463.

Fögen, T. 2007. "Pliny the Elder's Animals: Some Remarks on the Narrative Structure of *Nat. Hist.* 8–11", *Hermes 135*, no. 2: 184–198.

———. 2009. *Wissen, Kommunikation und Selbstdarstellung. Zur Struktur und Charakteristik römischer Fachtexte der frühen Kaiserzeit*. München.

———. 2010a. "Plinius der Altere zwischen Tradition und Innovation. Zur 'Ideologie' der *Naturalis Historia*", in N. Kramer and C. Reitz (eds.), *Tradition und Erneuerung. Mediale Strategien in der Zeit der Flavier*. Berlin and New York, 41–61.

————. 2010b. "Zur Rolle des Fachwortschatzes in der *Naturalis Historia* des Älteren Plinius", in A. Immhausen and T. Pommerening (eds.), *Writings of Early Scholars in Ancient Near East, Egypt, Rome, and Greece*. Berlin and New York, 93–118.

————. 2013. "Scholarship and Competitiveness: Pliny the Elder's Attitude towards His Predecessors in the *Naturalis Historia*", in M. Asper (ed.), *Writing Science: Medical and Mathematical Authorship in Ancient Greece*. Berlin and Boston, 83–107.

Fontijn, D.R. 2013. "Epilogue: Cultural Biographies and Itineraries of Things: Second Thoughts", in H.P. Hahn and H. Weis (eds.), *Mobility, Meaning and the Transformations of Things*. Oxford, 183–195.

Formarier, M. "Ρυθμός, *rhythmos* et *numerus* chez Cicéron et Quintilien. Perspectives esthétiques et génériques sur le rythme oratoire", *Rhetorica* 31, no. 2: 133–149.

Freestone, I.C. 2008. "Pliny on Roman Glassmaking", in M. Martinon-Torres and T. Rehren (eds.), *Archaeology, History and Science*. London and Walnut Creek, CA, 77–100.

French, R., and Greenaway, F. (eds.) 1986. *Science in the Early Roman Empire: Pliny the Elder, His Sources and Influence*. Totowa, NJ.

Fuhrer, T. 2014. "La dédicace littéraire et la mise en scène de l'auteur", in J.-C. Julhe (ed.), *Pratiques latines de la dédicace*. Paris, 215–240.

Gage, J. 1981. "A *locus classicus* of Colour Theory: the Fortunes of Apelles", *JWI* 44: 1–26.

Gahtan, M.W., and Pegazzano, D. (eds.) 2015. *Museum Archetypes and Collecting in the Ancient World*. Leiden.

Gaifman, M., and Platt, V. 2018. "Introduction: From Grecian Urn to Embodied Object", in M. Gaifman and V. Platt (eds.), *The Embodied Object in Classical Antiquity, Art History* 41, no. 3: 403–419.

Gaillard-Seux, P. 2003. "Sympathie et antipathie dans l'*Histoire Naturelle* de Pline l'Ancien", in N. Palmieri (ed.), *Rationnel et irrationnel dans la médecine ancienne et médiévale*. Saint-Étienne, 113–128.

Gallia, A.B. 2016. "Remaking Rome", in Zissos 2016, 148–165.

García Morcillo, M. 2008. "Performing Power and Authority at Roman Auctions", *AncSoc* 38: 185–213.

————. 2010. "Zwischen Kunst und *luxuria*: die korintischen Bronzen in Plinius' *Naturalis Historia*", *Hermes* 138, no. 4: 442–454.

Giannecchini, G. 1981–1982. "La sfera semantica di *numerus*", *AFLPer(class)* 19: 83–101.

Gibson, R. 2007. "Starting with the Index in Pliny", in L. Jansen (ed.), *The Roman Paratext: Frame, Text, Readers*. Cambridge, 33–55.

Gibson, R., and Morello, R. (eds.) 2011. *Pliny the Elder: Themes and Contexts*. Leiden and Boston.

Giglioni Bodei, G. 1974. *Lavori pubblici e occupazione nell'antichità classica*. Bologna.

Giuliano, A. 1989. *I Cammei della Collezione Medicea del Museo Archeologico di Firenze*. Roma.

Gleason, K.L. 2019. "The Lost Dimension: Pruned Plants in Roman Gardens", *Vegetation History and Archaeobotany* 28, no. 3: 311–325.

Gleason, K.L., Palmer, M.A., Allen, E., and Bai, L. 2020. "The Digital *Topiarius*: Toward a Method of Reconstructing the *Viridarium* of the Great Peristyle of the Villa Arianna at *Stabiae*", in A. Anguissola, M. Iadanza, and R. Olivito (eds.), *Paesaggi domestici. L'esperienza della natura nelle case e nelle ville romane*. Roma, 159–173.

Godsen, C., and Marshall, Y. (eds.) 1999. "The Cultural Biography of Objects", *World Archaeology* 31, no. 2: 169–178.

Goffen, R. 2001. "Signatures: Inscribing Identity in Italian Renaissance Art", *Viator* 32: 303–370.

Grethlein, J. 2017. *Aesthetic Experiences and Classical Antiquity*. Cambridge.

Gros, P. 1978. "Vie et mort de l'art hellénistique selon Vitruve et Pline", *REL*: 289–313 (= *Vitruve et la tradition des traités d'architecture*. Roma, 2006, 113–137).

———. 1989. "Les fondements philosophiques de l'harmonie architecturale selon Vitruve (*De architectura* III-IV)", *Journal of the Faculty of Letters. The University of Tokyo. Aesthetics* 14: 13–22 (= *Vitruve et la tradition des traités d'architecture*. Roma, 2006, 271–280).

———. 1997. *Vitruvio, De Architectura*, 2 vols., ed. by P. Gros, with translations and commentaries by A. Corso and E. Romano. Torino.

Gruen, E.S. 1993. *Culture and National Identity in Republican Rome*. London.

Gualandi, G. 1982. "Plinio e il collezionismo d'arte", in *Plinio il Vecchio sotto il profilo storico e letterario*. Como, 259–298.

Guipponi-Gineste, M.-F. 2010. *Claudien. Poète du monde à la cour d'Occident*. Paris.

———. 2011. "Pierres précieuses et pierres curieuses dans la poésie de Claudien", in F. Garambois-Vasquez (ed.), *Claudien. Mythe, histoire et science*. Saint-Étienne, 85–111.

Gutzwiller, K. 2004. "Seeing Thought: Timomachus' *Medea* and Ekphrastic Epigram", *AJPh* 125: 339–386.

———. (ed.) 2005. *The New Posidippus. A Hellenistic Poetry Book*. Oxford.

Gwilt, J. 1826. *The Architecture of Marcus Vitruvius Pollio in Ten Books*, transl. by Joseph Gwilt. London.

Hahn, C., and Shalem, A. (eds.) 2020. *Seeking Transparency. Rock Crystals across the Medieval Mediterranean*. Berlin.

Harari, M. 2000a. "Plinio il Vecchio e la storia dell'arte antica", in Pliny-Ferri 2000, 7–23.

———. 2000b. "Silvio Ferri e Plinio il Vecchio", in Pliny-Ferri 2000, 25–39.

———. 2002. "*Mimesis* e *thanatos*. Plinio il Vecchio e la fine dell'arte", *RSI* 114, no. 3, 756–773.

Hardiman, C. 2012. "Popular Aesthetics and Personal Art Appreciation in the Hellenistic Age", in I. Sluiter and R.M. Rosen (eds.), *Aesthetic Value in Classical Antiquity*. Leiden, 265–284.

Harich-Schwarzbauer, H. 2009. "*Prodigiosa silex*: Serielle Lektüre der *Carmina minora* Claudians", in H. Harich-Schwarzbauer and P. Shierl (eds.), *Lateinische Poesie der Spätantike*. Basel, 11–31.

Hauser, F. 1905. "Plinius und das censorische Verzeichnis", *MDAI(R)* 20: 206–213.

Healy, J.F. 1999. *Pliny the Elder on Science and Technology*. Oxford and New York.

Hegener, N. 2013. *"Faciebat, non finito* und andere Iperfekte Künstlersignaturen neben Michelangelo", in N. Hegener (ed.), *Künstler-Signaturen von der Antike bis zur Gegenwart*. Petersberg, 188–231.

Heile, I. 1990. "Licht und Dach beim griechischer Tempel", in W.-D. Heilmeyer and W. Hoepfner (eds.), *Licht und Architektur*. Tübingen, 27–34.

Henderson, J. 2011. "The Nature of Man: Pliny, *Historia Naturalis* as Cosmogram", *MD* 66: 139–171.

Hénin, E., and Naas, V. (eds.) 2018. *Le mythe de l'art antique entre anecdotes et lieux communs*. Paris.

Henke, F. 2020. "Gypsum, the Invention of Bronze Casting, and the Triumph of Form", in Anguissola and Grüner 2020, 145–156.

Hoepfner, W. 2001. "Der parische Lichtdom", *Antike Welt* 32, no. 5, 491–506.

Horn, H.-J. 1989. "Stoische Symmetrie und Theorie des Schönen in der Kaiserzeit", in *ANRW,* II, 36.3, 1454–1472.

Hoskins, J. 2006. "Agency, Biography and Objects", in C. Tilley, W. Keane, S. Küchler, M. Rowlands, and P. Spyer (eds.), *Handbook of Material Culture*. London, 74–84.

Howe, N.P. 1985. "In Defence of the Encyclopaedic Mode: On Pliny's Preface to the *Natural History*", *Latomus* 44: 561–576.

Hrychuk Kontokosta, A. 2019. "Building the *Thermae Agrippae*: Private Life, Public Space, and the Politics of Bathing in Early Imperial Rome", *AJA* 123, no. 1: 45–77.

Hulme, B.J. 2011. *"Naturalis Historiae* 37.3–4: Pliny, Livia, and the Sardonyx of Polycrates", *Phoenix* 65, no. 3–4: 395–397.

Hurley, D.W. 2013. "Biographies of Nero", in Buckley and Dinter 2013, 29–44.

Ibrahim, L., Scranton, R., and Brill, R. 1976. *Kenchreai Eastern Port of Corinth*, II. Leiden.

Isager, J. 1991. *Pliny on Art and Society*. Odense.

———. 2006a. "The Whole World Gathered in One Place. Pliny's Vision of Rome as a Museum", *AAAH* 20, no. 6: 65–78.

———. 2006b. "Pliny's *Natural History*: A Medium for Preservation and a Cause of Loss of Knowledge", *Classica* 19, no. 1: 115–125.

Jacobson, D.M., and Weitzman, M.P. 1995. "Black Bronze and the Corinthian Alloy", *CQ* 45: 580–583.

Jansen, C. 2016. "Accidental Harm Under (Roman) Civil Law", in K. Landsman and E. van Wolde (eds.), *The Challenge of Chance*. Cham, 233–247.

Jones, N.B. 2019. *Painting, Ethics, and Aesthetics in Rome*. Cambridge.

Jones-Lewis, M.A. 2012. "Poison: Nature's Argument for the Roman Empire in Pliny the Elder's *Naturalis Historia*", *CW* 106, no. 1: 51–74.

Kellum, B.A. 1990. "The City Adorned: Programmatic Display at the Aedes Concordiae Augustae", in K.A. Raaflaub and M. Toher (eds.), *Between Republic and Empire: Interpretations of Augustus and his Principate*. Berkeley.

Ker, J. 2004. "Nocturnal Writers in Imperial Rome: The Culture of *Lucubratio*", *CPh* 33, no. 3, 209–242.

Kleingünther, A. 1933. *ΠΡΩΤΟΣ ΕΥΡΕΤΗΣ. Untersuchungen zur Geschichte einer Fragestellung.* Leipzig.

Koch, N.J. 2000. *Techne und Erfindung in der Klassischen Malerei.* München.

———. 2000–2003. "ΣΧΗΜΑ. Zur Interferenz technischer Begriffe in Rhetorik und Kunstschriftstellerei", *IJCT* 6, no. 4: 503–515.

König, J., and Whitmarsh, T. 2007. "Ordering Knowledge", in J. König and T. Whitmarsh (eds.), *Ordering Knowledge in the Roman Empire.* Cambridge, 3–39.

König, J., and Woolf, G. (eds.) 2013a. *Encyclopaedism from Antiquity to the Renaissance.* Cambridge.

König, J., and Woolf, G. 2013b. "Introduction", in König and Woolf 2013a, 1–20.

Kopytoff, I. 1986. "The Cultural Biography of Things: Commoditization as Process", in A. Appadurai (ed.), *The Social Life of Things.* Cambridge, 64–91.

Kosmetatou, E. 2004. "Vision and Visibility: Art Historical Theory Paints a Portrait of New Leadership in Posidippus' *Andriantopoiika*", in Acosta-Hughes, Kosmetatou, and Baumbach 2004.

Köves-Zulauf, T. 1973. "Die Vorrede der plinianischen Naturgeschichte", *WS* 86: 134–184.

Krug, A. 1987. "Neros Augenglas: Realia zu einer Anekdote", in *Archéologie et médecine.* Juan-les-Pins, 459–475.

Kurz, D. 1970. *Akribeia. Das Ideal der Exaktheit bei den Griechen bis Aristoteles.* Göppingen.

Laehn, T.R. 2013. *Pliny's Defense of Empire.* New York and London.

Landucci, F. 2019. "Duride di Samo e la storia dell'arte antica: il contributo di un intellettuale poliedrico", in Adornato, Falaschi, and Poggio 2019, 123–134.

Lao, E. 2011. "Luxury and the Creation of a Good Consumer", in Gibson and Morello 2011, 35–56.

———. 2016. "Taxonomic Organization in Pliny's *Natural History*", in F. Cairns and R. Gibson (eds.), *Papers of the Langford Latin Seminar* 16: 209–246.

La Regina, A. 1991. "*Tabulae signorum urbis Romae*", in M.R. Di Mino (ed.), *Rotunda Diocletiani.* Roma, 3–8.

La Rocca, E. 1998. "Artisti rodii negli *horti* romani", in M. Cima and E. La Rocca (eds.), *Horti Romani.* Roma, 203–274.

———. 2001. "La nuova immagine dei fori imperiali", *MDAI(R)* 108: 171–213.

———. 2016. "Sulla bottega di Pasiteles e Stephanos, 2. Le *Appiades* di Stephanos nei *monumenta Asinii* e nel foro di Cesare", in E. Mangani and A. Pellegrino (eds.), *Για το φίλο μας. Scritti in ricordo di Gaetano Messineo.* Monte Compatri, 207–224.

———. 2017a. "Staging Nero: Public Imagery and the *Domus Aurea*", in Bartsch, Freudenburg, and Littlewood 2017, 195–212.

————. 2017b. "Sulla bottega di Pasiteles e di Stephanos. I. Il gruppo di Oreste e Elettra da Pozzuoli e il concetto di serialità", in L. Cicala and B. Ferrara (eds.), *Kithon Lydios*. Napoli, 875–895.

Lassen, H. 1995. "The Improved Product: A Philological Investigation of a Contemporary Legend", *Contemporary Legend* 5: 1–37.

Leen, A. 1991. "Cicero and the Rhetoric of Art", *AJPh* 112, no. 2: 229–245.

Lefons, C. 2000. *Gaio Plinio Secondo, Storia naturale. Libro XXXVII: gemme e pietre preziose*, with translation and notes by C. Lefons. Livorno.

Lehoux, D. 2012. *What Did the Romans Know? An Inquiry into Science and Worldmaking*. Chicago and London.

Libonati, E. 2017. "An Aspect of the Object Habit: Pliny the Elder, Audience and Politics", *Museum History Journal* 10, no. 2: 127–139.

Li Causi, P. 2010. "I generi dei generi (e le specie): le marche di classificazione di secondo livello dei romani e la zoologia di Plinio il Vecchio', *Annali Online di Ferrara. Lettere* 2: 107–142. <http://annali.unife.it/lettere/article/view/222/171> (last accessed 1st September 2020).

Lindberg, D.C. 1976. *Theories of Vision from Al-Kindi to Kepler*. Chicago: University of Chicago Press.

Lloyd, G.E.R. 1983. *Science, Folklore and Ideology: Studies in the Life Sciences in Ancient Greece*. Cambridge.

Lloyd, R.B. 1982. "Three Monumental Gardens on the Marble Plan", *AJA* 86: 91–100.

Locher, A. 1986. "The Structure of Pliny the Elder's *Natural History*", in French and Greenaway 1986, 20–29.

Lowe, D. 2010. "The Symbolic Value of Grafting in Ancient Rome", *TAPhA* 140: 461–488.

Macaulay-Lewis, E. 2011. "The City in Motion: Walking for Transport and Leisure in the City of Rome", in R. Laurence and D.J. Newsome (eds.), *Rome, Ostia, Pompeii*. Oxford, 262–289.

Malaspina, E. 2020. "Sul significato di *circumlitio*: nota a Seneca, *epist.* 86, 6, Plinio, *nat.* 35, 133 e Quint. 8, 5, 26", *BStudLat* 50, no. 1: 156–178.

Manolaraki, E.H. 2015. "*Hebraei Liquores*: The Balsam of Judaea in Pliny's *Natural History*", *AJPh* 136, no. 4: 633–667.

————. 2018. "Senses and the Sacred in Pliny's *Natural History*", *ICS* 43, no. 1, 207–233.

Manzoni, G.E. 1986. "Arcaismi e grecismi nella lingua della *Naturalis Historia*", in P.V. Cova, R. Gazich, G.E. Manzoni, and G. Melzani (eds.), *Studi sulla lingua di Plinio il Vecchio*. Milano, 171–200.

Marconi, C. (ed.) 2015. *The Oxford Handbook of Greek and Roman Art and Architecture*. Oxford and New York.

McFerrin, N. 2019. "Masks, Mirrors, and Mediated Perception: Reflective Viewing in the House of the Gilded Cupids", *Arts* 8.83 <doi: 10.3390/arts8030083> (last accessed 1st September 2020).

McHam, S.B. 2013. *Pliny and the Artistic Culture of the Italian Renaissance*. New Haven.

Megow, W.R. 1993. "Zum Florentiner Tituskameo", *AA*: 401–408.

Melina, G. 2007. "Plinio il Vecchio e la sua storia dell'arte antica", *Ars et Humanitas*: 127–150.

Merleau-Ponty, M. 2007. "Eye and Mind", in T. Toadvine and L. Lawlor (eds.), *The Merleau-Ponty Reader*. Evanston, 351–378.

Mette, H.J. 1960. "ΕΓΚΥΚΛΙΟΣ ΠΑΙΔΕΙΑ", *Gymnasium* 67: 300–307.

Michel, A. 1987. "L'esthétique de Pline l'Ancien", in Pigeaud and Oroz 1987, 371–383.

Miles, M. 2002. "Cicero's Prosecution of Gaius Verres: A Roman View of the Ethics of Acquisition of Art", *International Journal of Cultural Property* 11, no. 1: 28–49.

———. 2008. *Art as Plunder: The Ancient Origins of Debate about Cultural Property*. Cambridge.

Morello, R. 2011. "Pliny and the Encyclopaedic Addressee", in Gibson and Morello 2011, 147–165.

Morton, A.G. 1986. "Pliny on Plants: His Place in the History of Botany", in French and Garraway 1986, 86–97.

Moussy, C. 1966. *Gratia et sa famille*. Paris.

Mudry, P. 2004. "*Mirabilia* et *Magica*. Essai de définition dans l'*Histoire Naturelle*", in Mudry, Bianchi, and Thévanaz 2004, 239–252.

Mudry, P., Bianchi, O., and Thévanaz, O. (eds.) 2004. *Mirabilia. Conceptions et Répresentations de l'extraordinaire dans le monde antique*. Bern.

Murphy, T. 2003. "Pliny's *Naturalis Historia*: The Prodigal Text", in Boyle and Dominik 2003, 301–322.

———. 2004. *Pliny the Elder's Natural History. The Empire in the Encyclopedia*. Oxford and New York.

Naas, V. 1996. "L'art grec dans l'*Histoire naturelle* de Pline l'Ancien", *Histoire de l'art* 35–36: 15–26.

———. 2001. "*Et in his quidem, tametsi mirabilis, aliqua ratio* (*NH*, IX, 178): modes de construction du savoir et imaginaires de Pline l'Ancien", in M. Courrent and J. Thomas (eds.), *Imaginaire et modes de construction du savoir antique dans les textes scientifiques et techniques*. Perpignan, 15–33.

———. 2002. *Le projet encyclopédique de Pline l'Ancien*. Roma.

———. 2004. "*Opera mirabilia in terris* et *Romae operum miracula* dans l'*Histoire naturelle* de Pline l'Ancien", in Mudry, Bianchi, and Thévanaz 2004, 253–264.

———. 2006. "*Omnia ergo meliora fuere, cum minor copia* (Pline l'Ancien, *NH*, XXXV, 50): matières et couleurs au service d'un discours moral dans la minéralogie de Pline l'Ancien", in A. Rouveret, S. Dubel, and V. Naas (eds.), *Couleurs et matières dans l'antiquité*. Paris, 201–211.

———. 2008. "Pline l'Ancien a-t-il cru à ses mythes?", *Pallas* 78: 133–151.

———. 2011a. "Imperialism, *Mirabilia* and Knowledge. Some Paradoxes in the *Naturalis Historia*", in Gibson and Morello 2011, 57–70.

———. 2011b. "Philhellénisme et identité romaine chez Pline l'Ancien (*nat.* 7,81–130)", in A. Bonadeo, A. Canobbio, and F. Gasti (eds.), *Filellenismo e identità romana in età flavia*. Pavia, 35–58.

———. 2012a. "Anecdote et théorie de l'art chez Pline l'Ancien", in E. Hénin, F. Lecercle, and L. Wajeman (eds.), *La théorie subreptice. Les anecdotes dans la théorie de l'art (XVIe-XVIIIe siècles)*. Turnhout, 39–52.

———. 2012b. "Révélation et apprentissage dans l'*Histoire naturelle* de Pline l'Ancien", in A.N. Pena (ed.), *Révélation et apprentissage dans les textes grecs et latins*. Lisboa, 229–240.

———. 2013. "*Indicare, non indagare*: encyclopédisme contre histoire naturelle chez Pline", in A. Zucker (ed.), *Encyclopédire. Formes de l'ambition encyclopédique dans l'Antiquité et au Moyen-Âge*. Turnhout, 145–166.

———. 2016. "Douris de Samos chez Pline l'Ancien", in V. Naas and M. Simon (eds.), *De Samos à Rome: personnalité et influence de Douris*. Paris, 243–256.

———. 2019. "Aux origines de l'*Histoire Naturelle*: sources et structure de l'inventaire plinien", in A. Cohen-Skalli (ed.), *Historiens et érudits à leur écritoire*. Bordeaux, 225–242.

Nichols, M.F. 2017. *Author and Audience in Vitruvius' De Architectura*. Cambridge.

Nicolet, C. 1991. *Space, Geography, and Politics in the Early Roman Empire*. Ann Arbor, MI.

Nikitinski, O. 1998. "Plinius der Ältere. Seine Enzyklopädie und ihre Leser", in W. Kullmann, J. Althoff, and M. Asper (eds.), *Gattungen wissenschaftlicher Literatur in der Antike*. Tübingen, 341–359.

Noreña, C.F. 2003, "Medium and Message in Vespasian's Templum Pacis", *MAAR* 48: 25–43.

Ohnesorg, A. 1993. *Inselionische Marmordächer*. Berlin and New York.

———. 2011. "Der naxische Lichtdom. Das Phänomen lichtdurchlässiger inselionischer Marmordächer", in P.I. Schneider and U. Wulf-Rheidt (eds.), *Licht- Konzepte in der vormodernen Architektur*. Regensburg, 92–100.

Olick, J.K., Vinitzky-Seroussi, V., and Levy, D. (eds.) 2011. *The Collective Memory Reader*. Oxford and New York.

Osgood, J. 2006. *Caesar's Legacy. Civil War and the Emergence of the Roman Empire*. Cambridge.

Östenberg, I. 2009. *Staging the World: Spoils, Captives, and Representations in the Roman Triumphal Procession*. Oxford.

Packer, J.E. 2003. "Parsing Flavian Rome", in Boyle and Dominik 2003, 175–198.

Paparazzo, E. 2011. "Philosophy and Science in the *Naturalis Historia*", in Gibson and Morello 2011, 89–111.

Papini, M. 2017. "Firmare un'opera come se fosse l'ultima: l'imperfetto e l'incompiuto in Plinio il Vecchio", *BCAR* 118: 39–54.

———. 2018. "Il Canone di Policleto", *Lexicon Philosophicum*: 5–41.

———. 2019. "*Pendono interrotte le opere*". *Antichi monumenti incompiuti nel mondo greco*. Roma.

———. 2020. "*Pretia* and *auctoritas rerum*. Evaluation of Materials and Artefacts in Books 33–37", in Anguissola and Grüner 2020, 181–193.

Pascucci, G. 1980. "La lettera prefatoria di Plinio alla *Naturalis Historia*", *InvLuc* 2: 5–39.

————. 1982. "La lettera prefatoria di Plinio alla *Naturalis Historia*", in *Plinio il Vecchio sotto il profilo storico e letterario*. Como, 171–197.

Pérez González, J. 2019. "Gems in Ancient Rome: Pliny's Vision", *SCI* 38: 139–151.

Pernot, L. 1993. *La rhétorique de l'éloge dans le monde gréco-romain*, I. Paris.

Perry, E.E. 2000. "Notes on *Diligentia* as a Term of Roman Art Criticism", *CPh* 95: 445–458.

————. 2005. *The Aesthetics of Emulation in the Visual Arts of Ancient Rome*. Cambridge.

Petrain, D. 2005. "Gems, Metapoetics, and Value: Greek and Roman Responses to a Third-Century Discourse on Precious Stones", *TAPhA* 135, no. 2, 329–357.

Pià Comella, J. 2014. *Une piété de la raison. Philosophie et religion dans le stoïcisme impérial*. Turnhout.

Pigeaud, J. 1987. "La rêverie de la limite dans la peinture antique", in Pigeaud and Oroz 1987, 413–430.

Pigeaud, J., and Oroz, J. (eds.) 1987. *Pline l'Ancien, temoin de son temps*. Salamanca.

Pinkster, H. 2005. "The Language of Pliny the Elder", in T. Reinhardt, M. Lapidge, and J.N. Adams (eds.), *Aspects of the Language of Latin Prose*. Oxford, 239–256.

Plantzos, D. 1997. "Crystals and Lenses in the Graeco-Roman World", *AJA* 101, no. 3: 451–464.

Platt, V.J. 2010. "Art History in the Temple", *Arethusa* 43, no. 2: 197–213.

————. 2016a. "The Artist as Anecdote: Creating Creators in Ancient Texts and Modern Art History", in R. Fletcher and J. Hanink (eds.), *Creative Lives in Classical Antiquity*. Cambridge, 274–304.

————. 2016b. "The Matter of Classical Art History", *Daedalus* 145, no. 2: 69–78.

————. 2018a. "Ecology, Ethics and Aesthetics in Pliny the Elder's *Natural History*", *Journal of the Clark Art Institute* 17: 219–242.

————. 2018b. "Of Sponges and Stones: Matter and Ornament in Roman Painting", in N. Dietrich and M. Squire (eds.), *Ornament and Figure*. Berlin and Boston, 241–278.

————. 2018c. "Orphaned Objects: The Phenomenology of the Incomplete in Pliny's *Natural History*", in M. Gaifman, V. Platt, and M. Squire (eds.), *The Embodied Object in Classical Antiquity, Art History* 41, no. 3: 493–517.

————. 2020a. "Beeswax: The Natural History of an Archetypal Medium", in Anguissola and Grüner 2020, 51–64.

————. 2020b. "The Seal of Polycrates: A Discourse on Discourse Channel Conditions", in P. Michelakis (ed.), *Classics and Media Theory*. Oxford, 53–76.

Platt, V.J. and Squire, M. 2013. "Getting to Grips with Classical Art: Rethinking the Haptics of Graeco-Roman Visual Culture", in A. Purves (ed.), *Touch and the Ancient Senses*. London, 75–104.

Platz-Horster, G. 2012. *Erhabene Bilder. Die Kameen in der Antikensammlung Berlin.* Wiesbaden: Reichert.

Poggio, A. 2018. "Experiencing Art in the *Saepta*. Greek Artworks in a Monumental Space of Ancient Rome", in Adornato, Romano, Cirucci, and Poggio 2018, 191–207.

———. 2019. "Mappare Plinio. Opere d'arte nella Roma di età imperiale", in Adornato, Falaschi, and Poggio 2019, 217–232.

———. 2020. "Accumulating and Interacting. Artworks in Ancient Rome's Public Spaces", in Adornato, Cirucci, and Cupperi 2020, 113–121.

Polansky, R. 2010. *Aristotle's De Anima: A Critical Commentary.* Cambridge.

Pollard, E.A. 2009. "Pliny's *Natural History* and the Flavian *Templum Pacis*: Botanical Imperialism in First-Century CE Rome", *Journal of World History* 20: 309–338.

Pollitt, J.J. 1974. *The Ancient View of Greek Art.* New Haven and London.

———. 1978. "The Impact of Greek Art on Rome", *TAPhA* 108: 155–174.

Porter, J.I. 2010. *The Origins of Aesthetic Thought in Ancient Greece.* Cambridge and New York.

———. 2011. "Against *leptotes*: Rethinking Hellenistic Aesthetics", in A. Erskine and L. Llewellyn-Jones (eds.), *Creating a Hellenistic World.* Swansea, 271–312.

Powers, J. 2011. "Beyond Painting in Pompeii's Houses: Wall Ornaments and Their Patrons", in E. Poehler, M. Flohr, and K. Cole (eds.), *Pompeii. Art, Industry and Infrastructure.* Oxford, 10–32.

Preisshofen, F. 1979. "Kunsttheorie und Kunstbetrachtung", in H. Flashar (ed.), *Le classicisme à Rome aux Iers siècles avant et après J.-C.* Vandœuvres, 262–277.

Pucci, G. 2004–2005. "Il *rhythmós* nell'arte figurativa greca", *Quaderni Warburg Italia* 2–3: 137–152.

Reitzenstein, D. 2016. "*Auri sanies*: Nero, Gold und *chrysocolla*", in K.B. Zimmer (ed.), *Von der Reproduktion zur Rekonstruktion.* Rahden, 115–133.

Riggsby, A.M. 1997. "Public and Private in Roman Culture: The Case of the *cubiculum*", *JRA* 10: 36–56.

———. 2007. "Guides to the Wor(l)d", in J. König and T. Whitmarsh (eds.), *Ordering Knowledge in the Roman Empire.* Cambridge, 88–107.

Robert, R. 1995. "*Immensa potentia artis.* Prestige et statut des oeuvres d'art à Rome à la fin de la République et au début de l'Empire", *RA*: 291–305.

———. 2013. "*Arte et amore captus.* Les collections: une appropriation controversée des *opera publica* et la perception du décor privé", in A. Dardenay and E. Rosso (eds.), *Dialogues entre sphère publique et sphère privée dans l'espace de la cité romaine.* Bordeaux, 235–250.

Roche, P. 2016. "Latin Prose Literature: Author and Authority in the Prefaces of Pliny and Quintilian", in Zissos 2016, 434–449.

Roddaz, H.-M. 1984. *Marcus Agrippa.* Roma.

Romani Mistretta, M. 2018. "Empire and Invention: The Elder Pliny's Heurematology (*Nat.* VII 191–215)", *ACD* 54: 123–135.

Romano, E. 2003. "Il lessico latino dei colori: il punto della situazione", in S. Beta and M.M. Sassi (eds.), *I colori nel mondo antico*. Fiesole, 41–53.

Romm, J.S. 1992. *The Edges of the Earth in Ancient Thought*. Princeton.

Rosati, G. 1997. "Profumo di terra: valori e simboli dell'immaginario romano", in A. Avanzini (ed.), *Profumi d'Arabia*. Roma, 515–528.

Rouveret, A. 1987a. "Toute la memoire du monde: la notion de collection dans la *NH* de Pline", *Helmantica* 38: 115–133.

———. 1987b. "Toute la memoire du monde: la notion de collection dans l'*Histoire Naturelle* de Pline", in Pigeaud and Oroz 1987, 431–449.

———. 1989. *Histoire et imaginaire de la peinture ancienne (Ve siècle av. J.-C.-Ier siècle ap. J.-C.)*. Roma.

———. 1996. "De l'artisan à l'artiste: quelques *topoi* des biographies antiques", in M. Waschek (ed.), *Les 'Vies' d'artistes*. Paris, 25–40.

———. 2007. "Ce que Pline l'Ancien dit de la peinture grecque: histoire de l'art ou éloge de Rome?", *CRAI* 151, no. 2: 619–632.

Rutledge, S.H. 2012. *Ancient Rome as a Museum*. Oxford.

Salvadori, M. 2016, "Alcune note sull'attività pittorica nel mondo romano: profili professionali, 'botteghe', tecniche particolari", in J. Bonetto, M.S. Busana, A.R. Ghiotto, M. Salvadori, and P. Zanovello (eds.), *I mille volti del passato*. Roma, 469–490.

Salvo, G. 2018. *Pinacothecae. Testimonianze di collezionismo di quadri nel mondo antico*. Roma.

Salway, B. 2001. "Travel, *Itineraria* and *Tabellaria*", in C. Adams and R. Laurence (eds.), *Travel and Geography in the Roman Empire*. London and New York, 22–66.

Sansone, D. 1993. "Nero's Final Hours", *ICS* 18: 179–189.

Santini, C. 1986. "Il vetro infrangibile (Petronio 51)", in *Semiotica della novella latina*. Roma, 117–124.

Sassi, M.M. 1994. "Critica dell'arte", in *EAA*, Suppl. 2: 327–331.

Schliesser, E. 2015. *Sympathy: A History*. Oxford: Oxford University Press. Oxford Scholarship Online. <doi: 10.1093/acprof:oso/9780199928873.001.0001> (last accessed 1st September 2020).

Schulz, V. 2019. *Deconstructing Imperial Representation. Tacitus, Cassius Dio, and Suetonius on Nero and Domitian*. Leiden and Boston.

Schultze, C. 2011. "Encyclopaedic Exemplarity in Pliny the Elder", in Gibson and Morello 2011, 167–186.

Schweitzer, B. 1932. *Xenokrates von Athen*. Halle.

Schwyzer, E. 1923. "Deutungsversuche griechischer, besonders homerischer Wörter", *Glotta* 12: 8–29.

Segenni, S. 2000. "Roma e le 'Laudes Italiae' in Plinio (Plin. *N.H.* 3, 65–68; 39–42)", *Acme* 53, no. 2: 273–277.

Settis, S. 1992. "La trattatistica delle arti figurative", in G. Cambiano, L. Canfora, and D. Lanza (eds.), *Lo spazio letterario della Grecia antica*, I.2. Roma, 469–498.

———. 1999. *Laocoonte. Fama e stile*. Roma: Donzelli.

Shaya, J. 2015. "Ancient Analogs of Museums", in E.A. Friedland, M. Sobo-cinski, and E.K. Gazda (eds.), *The Oxford Handbook of Roman Sculpture*. New York, 622–637.

Shields, C. 2016. Aristotle, *De Anima*, translated with introduction and commentary by C. Shields. Oxford.

Simmel, G. 1902. "Der Bildrahmen. Ein ästhetischer Versuch", *Der Tag* 541 (cited from "The Picture Frame: An Aesthetic Study", transl. by M. Ritter. *Theory, Culture, and Society* 11.1: 11–17).

Sinclair, P. 2003, "Rhetoric of Writing and Reading in the *Preface* to Pliny's *Natural History*", in Boyle and Dominik 2003, 277–299.

Smith, C. 2007. "Pliny the Elder and Archaic Rome", in Bispham and Rowe 2007, 147–170.

Smith, M.A. 1996. "Ptolemy's Theory of Visual Perception: An English Translation of the Optics with Introduction and Commentary", *TAPhS* 86, Part 2.

Serbat, G. 1973. "La reference comme indice de distance dans l'enonce de Pline l'Ancien", *RPh* 47: 38–49.

Sprigath, G. 2000. "Der Fall Xenokrates von Athen. Zu den Methoden der Antike-Rezeption in der Quellenforschung", in M. Baumbach (ed.), *Tradita et inventa: Beiträge zur Rezeption der Antike*. Heidelberg, 407–428.

Squire, M. 2017, "Framing the Roman 'Still Life': Campanian Wall-Painting and the Frames of Mural Make-Believe", in V. Platt and M. Squire (eds.), *The Frame in Classical Art*. Cambridge, 188–253.

Steiner, D. 2015. "Greek and Roman Theories of Art", in Marconi 2015, 21–40.

Stewart, P. 2003. *Statues in Roman Society*. Oxford.

Stoichita, V.I. 1997. *The Self-Aware Image: An Insight into Early Modern Meta-Painting*. Cambridge.

Syme, R. 1969. "Pliny the *Procurator*", *HSPh* 73: 201–236.

———. 1987. "Carrière et amis consulaires de Pline", *Helmantica* 38: 223–231.

Taborelli, L. 1991. "*Aromata* e *medicamenta* in Plinio (Parte Prima)", *Athanaeum* 79, no. 1: 527–562.

———. 1994. "*Aromata* e *medicamenta exotica* in Plinio (Parte Prima)", *Athanaeum* 82, no. 1: 111–151.

Tanner, J. 2006. *The Invention of Art History in Ancient Greece*. Cambridge.

Thibodeau, P. 2016. "Ancient Optics: Theories and Problems of Vision", in G.L. Irby (ed.), *A Companion to Science, Technology, and Medicine in Ancient Greece and Rome*. Chichester and Hoboken, NJ, 130–144.

Thorburn, J.E. Jr. 2008. "Suetonius' *Tiberius*: A Proxemic Approach", *CPh* 103, no. 4: 435–448.

Todd, R.B. 1974. "ΣΥΝΕΝΤΑΣΙΣ and the Stoic Theory of Perception", *GB* 2: 251–261.

Totelin, L. 2012. "Botanizing Rulers and their Herbal Subjects: Plants and Political Power in Greek and Roman Literature", *Phoenix* 66, no. 1–2: 122–144.

Tressaud, A., and Vickers, M. 2007. "Ancient Murrhine Ware and Its Glass Evocations", *Journal of Glass Studies* 49, 143–152.

Tucci, P.L. 2017. *The Temple of Peace in Rome*. Cambridge.

van der Veen, J.E. 1993. "The Lord of the Ring. Narrative Technique in Herodotus' Story on Polycrates' Ring", *Mnemosyne* 46, no. 4: 433–457.

Varner, E.R. 2004. *Mutilation and Transformation. Damnatio Memoriae and Roman Imperial Portraiture*. Leiden.

———. 2017. "Nero's Memory in Flavian Rome", in Bartsch, Freudenburg, and Littlewood 2017, 237–257.

Varone, A. and Béarat, H. 1997. "Pittori romani al lavoro. Materiali, strumenti, techniche: evidenze archeologiche e dati analitici di un recente scavo pompeiano lungo via dell'Abbondanza (*Reg.* IX *ins.* 12)", in H. Béarat, M. Fuchs, M. Maggetti, and D. Paunier (eds.), *Roman Wall Painting*. Fribourg, 199–206.

Vegetti, M. 1981. "Lo spettacolo della natura. Circo, teatro e potere in Plinio", *Aut-Aut* 184–185: 111–125.

Vial-Logeay, A. 2010. "L'autre de Rome? Quelques remarques sur l'île de Taprobane dans l'*Histoire Naturelle* de Pline l'Ancien", in M.-F. Marein, P. Voisin, and J. Gallego (eds.), *Figures de l'étranger autour de la Méditerranée antique*, Paris, 159–167.

———. 2017. "Délocaliser la culture? Quelques remarques sur l'*Histoire Naturelle* de Pline l'Ancien et la culture de son temps", in P. Ciprés (ed.), *Plinio el Viejo y la construcción de Hispania citerior*. Vitoria-Gasteiz, 15–31.

Voelke-Viscardi, G. 2001. "Les gemmes dans l'*Histoire naturelle* de Pline l'Ancien: discours et modes de fonctionnement de l'univers", *MH* 58, no. 2: 99–122.

Vout, C. 2017. "Art and the Decadent City", in Bartsch, Freudenburg, and Littlewood 2017, 179–194.

Wallace-Hadrill, A. 1990. "Pliny the Elder and Man's Unnatural History", *G&R* 37, no. 1: 80–96.

Wang, A.J. 2004. "Michelangelo's Signature", *The Sixteenth Century Journal* 35, no. 2: 447–473.

Weis, H.A. 2003. "Gaius Verres and the Roman Art Market: Consumption and Connoisseurship in Late Republican Rome", in A. Haltenhoff, A. Heil, and F.-H. Mutschler (eds.), *O tempora, O mores. Römische Werte und Römische Literatur in Den Letzten Jahrzehnten Der Republik*. München, 355–400.

Welch, K.E. 2007. *The Roman Amphitheatre*. Cambridge.

White, P. 1988. "Julius Caesar in Augustan Rome", *Phoenix* 42, no. 4: 334–356.

Wilson Jones, M. 2000. "Doric Measure and Architectural Design 1: The Evidence of the Relief from Salamis", *AJA* 104, no. 1: 73–93.

———. 2001. "Doric Measure and Architectural Design 2: A Modular Reading of the Classical Temple", *AJA* 105, no. 4: 675–713.

———. 2015. "Greek and Roman Architectural Theory", in Marconi 2015, 41–69.

Woods, D. 2006. "Pliny, Nero, and the 'Emerald' (*NH* 37,64)", *Arctos* 40: 189–196.

———. 2009. "Curing Nero: A Cold Drink in Context", *Classics Ireland* 16, no. 4: 40–48.

Wolf, E. 1955. "Zur Etymologie von ῥυθμός und seiner Bedeutung in der älteren griechischen Literatur", *WS* 68: 99–119.

Zanker, P. 1998. "Un'arte per i sensi. Il mondo figurativo di Dioniso e Afrodite", in S. Settis (ed.), *I Greci. Storia, Cultura, Arte Società*, II.3. Torino, 545–616.

Zehnacker, H. 1983. "Pline l'Ancien, lecteur d'Ovide et de Sénèque (*N.H.* XXXIII, 1–3)", in H. Zehnacker and G. Hentz (eds.), *Hommages à Robert Schilling*. Paris, 437–446.

———. 1987. "La description de Rome dans le livre 3 de la *NH*", in Pigeaud and Oroz 1987, 307–320.

Zimmer, G. 1985. "Schriftquellen zum antiken Bronzeguss", in H. Born (ed.), *Archäologische Bronzen*. Berlin, 38–50.

Zissos, A. (ed.) 2016. *A Companion to the Flavian Age of Imperial Rome*. Chichester and Malden.

Zwierlein-Diehl, E. 2008. *Magie der Steine. Die antiken Prunkkameen im Kunsthistorischen Museum*. Wien.

Index of passages from the Natural History

Note: Page numbers followed by "n" denote endnotes.

Index of Greek and Latin sources

Note: Page numbers followed by "n" denote endnotes.

General index

Note: Page numbers followed by "n" denote endnotes.

For Product Safety Concerns and Information please contact our EU
representative GPSR@taylorandfrancis.com
Taylor & Francis Verlag GmbH, Kaufingerstraße 24, 80331 München, Germany

www.ingramcontent.com/pod-product-compliance
Lightning Source LLC
Chambersburg PA
CBHW060856170526
45158CB00001B/372